François Laruelle's
Principles of Non-Philosophy
A Critical Introduction and Guide

ANTHONY PAUL SMITH

University Press

© Anthony Paul Smith, 2016

Edinburgh University Press Ltd
The Tun—Holyrood Road,
12(2f) Jackson's Entry,
Edinburgh EH8 8PJ

www.euppublishing.com

Typeset in 11/13pt Monotype Ehrhardt by
Iolaire Typesetting, Newtonmore, and
printed and bound in the United States of America

A CIP record for this book is available from the British Library

ISBN 978 0 7486 8526 4 (hardback)
ISBN 978 0 7486 8528 8 (webready PDF)
ISBN 978 0 7486 8527 1 (paperback)
ISBN 978 0 7486 8529 5 (epub)

The right of Anthony Paul Smith to be identified as the author of this work has been
asserted in accordance with the Copyright, Designs and Patents Act 1988,
and the Copyright and Related Rights Regulations 2003 (SI No. 2498).

Contents

Acknowledgments

Books are never the result of the author alone and this is especially true when it comes to books written on translations of other books. I am tempted to say that writing a book is something like translation all the way down. With that said, I first want to thank the two people most involved with the translation of *Principles of Non-Philosophy*: my co-translator Nicola Rubczak for helping me to think through the question of translation, and François Laruelle for always patiently answering my questions regarding his work. Thank you to Carol Macdonald and John Ó Maoilearca for suggesting the book, commissioning it, and providing encouragement during the writing process. Thank you also to Jenny Daly, Michelle Houston, and Holly Roberts at Edinburgh University Press for shepherding the project through production. Tim Clark's copy editing has made this a much better book and I appreciate the skill he brought to the task. Special thanks to Alice Rekab (whose intellectual and artistic work using non-philosophy I have found consistently interesting and inspiring), Michael O'Neill Burns (whose work on German Idealism and contemporary French philosophy goes far beyond mere historical work), and Marika Rose (for her appreciation of a good line and helping me to see what questions a new reader of Laruelle would have). All three read through the manuscript and suggested a number of improvements, for which I am most appreciative. Daniel Whistler graciously gave me his Liverpudlian apartment for a month allowing me to make significant progress on the manuscript. Thank you to Michael O'Rourke, Fintan Neylan, and Paul Ennis who invited me to participate in their Dublin Unit for Speculative Thought (DUST) lecture series, which gave me the opportunity to present an early version of Chapter 6. Thank you to Hannah Kovacs for her invitation to speak in The After-Life of Phenomenology Workshop,

Acknowledgments

sponsored by Northwestern University's Alice Kaplan Institute for the Humanities and the Department of Philosophy, where I presented an early version of Chapter 2. My colleagues in the Department of Religion at La Salle University, especially Jack Downey, Jordan Copeland, and Maureen O'Connell, were sources of encouragement when I found the balance between writing and teaching difficult and I feel very lucky to count such colleagues as friends. I acknowledge the financial support provided by Tom Keagy, Dean of the School of Arts and Sciences at La Salle University, and Maureen O'Connell, Chair of the Department of Religion, which allowed me to participate in the colloquium held at Cerisy in September of 2014 on Laruelle's non-standard philosophy, where I was lucky enough to spend a week with some of the most interesting and challenging French, Irish, English, American, and Russian readers of Laruelle and practitioners of non-philosophy. While French befuddlement concerning the vegetarian diet led to a number of meals consisting of only bread, mustard, and copious amounts of wine, the intellectual nourishment provided by my non-philosophical comrades more than made up for the lack of a full belly.

This book is dedicated to the translators of theoretical texts; our task is largely thankless and our goal is an impossibility, yet the work must be done. It is also dedicated to the dear memory of Maizie, who would provide me with companionship as she sat with me for hours as I researched and worked on the book. I very much miss editing out the additions she would make to my written work as she walked across my keys. I always supposed they were meaningless, but perhaps that was just another failure of translation.

Abbreviations

DNP   *Dictionary of Non-Philosophy*
EU   *En tant qu'Un*
IP   *Intellectuals and Power: The Insurrection of the Victim*
PD   *Philosophies of Difference: A Critical Introduction to Non-Philosophy*
PhNP   *Philosophy and Non-Philosophy*
PNP   *Principles of Non-Philosophy*
PNS   *Philosophie non-standard. Générique, Quantique, Philo-Fiction*
NM   *Introduction to Non-Marxism*
SU   *Struggle and Utopia at the End Times of Philosophy*
TI   *Théorie des identités. Fractalité généralisée et philosophie artificielle*

Introduction:
A Constellation, Not a Mirror – The Form of a Non-Philosophical Readers' Guide

What would a non-philosophical readers' guide and introduction look like? This was the question I asked myself when I was approached by Carol Macdonald at Edinburgh University Press to consider writing this critical guide and introduction to François Laruelle's *Principles of Non-Philosophy*, originally published in French in 1996 and in English translation in 2013. I have devoted a great deal of time to this text, having spent a number of years translating it alongside my friend and co-translator Nicola Rubczak. Translators have a truly horrifying task, one that I am unsure those who are not translators are really aware of. As Drew S. Burk (another co-translator and friend) claims, to translate is to assume that a text is legible, yet the translator is also embedded so deeply into the text that seeing and communicating that legibility becomes more complicated. For the text, through your translating, becomes part of your own thinking. The closeness of your production to the text makes that legibility clear to you, much in the same way ones own thoughts are themselves clear. Yet, at the same time, that legibility is also alien to you for it is not yours. While you may feel the text is close to you, you also have to respect that text and the way it was originally written by someone who is other than you. And other in a special way, because, at least often in the translation of philosophy and other theory, you assume a certain importance of this text that you would not necessarily assume of your own texts. The thinker being translated, you feel, ought to have a wider readership and so you have taken up the task of trying to make that possible in a language other than the mother tongue of the thinker being translated. And yet you are also more aware of the shortcomings of the text, much as you might be aware of those in your own writing, and you are aware of the shortcomings of the translation in

1

comparison to the original as some points resist a clear translation, an easy legibility. So you move from an understanding of the text as universally legible, as if it were a divine text, and you come to a real text, imperfect, with traces or intimations that cannot be captured in the new language, with the limitations of language, the limitations of translatability, and the demands of publishing that exist regardless of the philosophical importance and limitations of the text.

But if this is the case, then to be a translator is to be a reader who is aware. A reader that reads a text so deeply that they have re-written it word for word and yet also done so differently. It is in this mode, with this strange relation of familiarity and alienness, that I began to try and make sense of what a critical guide and introduction might look like from a non-philosophical perspective. In fact I only agreed to develop this guide because as the translator of the text I could see it being part of the wider process of a non-philosophical translation, aiming to fashion a clone of the original text rather than represent it. To translate this question into a more legible form for new readers we may ask, how can an introduction and guide present itself without sufficiency, without the self-sufficiency of a kind of history of philosophy? This is the sufficiency that would be present if you or I treated this introduction and guide as *the* introduction and guide, presenting itself as the way one *has* to approach *Principles of Non-Philosophy*. Instead, the answer may be that the introduction and guide must not present itself as a mirror of the text, it must not present itself as the reduction of the text into simpler images and examples, but instead expand and generalize the text it aims to guide readers through in the first place. Expand and generalize its legibility also where the text resists legibility in the original. For, at least here where the text in question is one of François Laruelle's, sometimes the goal is to think something that itself stretches the capacities of language and the boundaries of communicability.[1]

But it is my contention that expanding those moments of incommunicability is possible because they are written very clearly in Laruelle. He says in *Principles of Non-Philosophy* that non philosophy does what it says and says what it means. So my approach in this book has not been to shut down the individual reader's encounter with *Principles of Non-Philosophy*, but simply to lay out certain points that constitute a constellation within which *Principles of Non-Philosophy* functions. In standard philosophical terms, I have aimed in part to provide something like the scholarly apparatus implied but not explicitly found in *Principles of Non-Philosophy*. The reader of Laruelle's text will notice that there are none of the usual citations one is used to seeing, though there are clearly concepts and names running through the book that are plucked from the history of philosophy and European thought generally. Laruelle sees his own work as something very different from a work *on* that history of philosophy. He sees his own work as sitting down with material (philosophy in this case) and fashioning something new from it. But, in tracing that scholarly apparatus, I am not aiming to provide all of the footnotes and citations which Laruelle elides when he claims he is not doing the history of philosophy but philosophy itself. Rather, I discuss the figures as well as the concepts that these names (Kant, Fichte, Husserl, Althusser, Henry, Marion, etc.) index and that form the material for Laruelle in *Principles of Non-Philosophy*. This introduction and guide does not then primarily explicate Laruelle's concepts in the same way that he does, though it will of course trace their shape but in such a way as to show the reader where he or she may find a handhold or a foothold as they approach the original text. This guide should not be read as a replacement for *Principles of Non-Philosophy*, but as another tool to be used as you work through that text. Towards that end, it will provide the reader with a map of the constellation of themes, the general shape of concepts, and the influence of other thinkers that guide and structure the original text. This will help the reader to read what Laruelle has written, to see what Laruelle is doing, rather than being presented with something like an authoritative reading of the work that would only point back towards its own authority.[2]

While in *Principles of Non-Philosophy* the reader will find only a single original footnote by Laruelle – and this only to signal the work of his friend Serge Valdinoci called "europanalysis" – there are still clear concepts and images freely taken and used from a plethora of establishment and radical philosophers: Plato, Spinoza, Kant, Heidegger, Wittgenstein, Derrida, Deleuze, Badiou, and even those further afield from classical philosophical practice like Gödel and Lacan. Perhaps though, the most important framing points are Marxian philosophy as developed by Marx and Louis Althusser, Husserlian phenomenology as it was developed in France by Jean-Luc Marion and Michel Henry, and the idealism of Fichte, whose *Science of Knowledge* is explicitly adapted and mutated. The first two, Marxism and phenomenology, are especially important in understanding the style of the text, since, for Laruelle, it is thinkers in these traditions who have taken the notion of a scientific philosophy the furthest. Both traditions, however, err in their own way: Marx goes too far towards empiricism and Husserl too far towards transcendentalism. But their efforts, even as philosophers, have to be respected even if through a kind of non-philosophical indifference towards the use of these names as authorities or "Great Men of Philosophy." That respect takes the form of drawing materials from both that come to form the core concepts of non-philosophy, albeit in mutated form: namely the Husserlian question of what a subject is alongside the question of phenomenology's investigation of epistemology (how we know) and subjectivity, and the development of the Marxist concept of determination in the last instance as a theory of causality, alongside a development of Fichte's radicalization of Kant's *Critique of Pure Reason* in his philosophy of a priori knowledge or, as one translation would have us use the gerund to indicate its lived quality, a priori knowing.

Phenomenology has a special place in terms of what we could term the literary style of the text. In our translators' preface to *Principles of Non-Philosophy*, Rubczak and I situate the text in relation to the original series in which it was published. That series, titled *Épitméthée* (the French name for the Greek titan Epimetheus, brother to Prometheus), is the home of a number of important texts in phenomenology, and Laruelle plays with that tradition in *Principles of Non-Philosophy* in a way we do not see as forcefully elsewhere. However, while Laruelle make use of this tradition he does so without making himself a standard phenomenologist in any meaningful sense; instead he shows the way in which phenomenology may be a material with which different theoretical pursuits can be undertaken. In a certain way phenomenology simply becomes a means by which he can develop non-philosophy. As is also common with Laruelle, he plays on the writing style of Husserl and Henry a bit throughout the text, taking up the vocabulary of phenomenology and crafting sentences that turn in on themselves. *Principles of Non-Philosophy* lays out the fundamental aspects of non-philosophy's method by ventriloquizing or pantomiming the phenomenological tradition alongside a Marxist supplement of equal and critical importance.[3] So, non-philosophy's main concepts are discussed through themes familiar to those who have studied the phenomenological tradition, themes like noema and noesis, the ego and the cogito, and the relationship of the intentionality of thought to objects in the world. But these are all modified under the traditionally Marxist problematic of determination in the last instance, which subjects each theme to this unilateral relationship (the meaning of unilaterality will be explained in detail in Chapter 4).[4] Part of our task in this book will be to explain these terms, familiar for some and foreign for others, which have been translated into non-philosophy by Laruelle. However, just as I have not envisioned this text as a replacement for *Principles of Non-Philosophy*, I have also not intended it to be a translation of the text into a simpler idiom. As a thinker who has made use of Laruelle's non-philosophy for my own purposes, I recognize how antithetical to his project such an attempt would prove. Readers should thus be aware that not all of the important terms are explicated, and for those that are, the way in which they are explicated lays no claim to any special knowledge of Laruelle's internal thought processes. The guide is simply offered as the work of a reader who is aware of and may point to certain elements of the path that those new to it may not be able to see.

As phenomenology has taught us, such perception is always partial and undoubtedly obscures other elements. If this guide and introduction helps those who read the text and find other ways to traverse it I will be able to consider it a success.

Allow me here to summarize the chapters that follow. While I have structured each chapter to build on the preceding ones, the reader may wish to skip around based on their own familiarity with *Principles of Non-Philosophy* or the non-philosophical project generally. Each chapter of this guide corresponds to the same numbered chapter in *Principles of Non-Philosophy* (thus this introduction corresponds to the "Introduction" in *Principles of Non-Philosophy*, though Chapter 1 touches on elements from both Laruelle's introduction and his first chapter). Chapters 1 to 3 foreground Laruelle's project by explicating it in relation to other figures whose importance to Laruelle is clear but not focused upon in *Principles of Non-Philosophy*. In Chapters 4 and 5 the focus is on the structure of the concepts, with occasional reference to the influences and sources when this seemed useful in elucidating the concept. Chapter 6 presented a special challenge, since the corresponding chapter in *Principles of Non-Philosophy* runs to seventy-one pages and aims to delineate in detail the highly abstract field that Laruelle's earlier chapters had only sought to prepare for. Upon considering how best to present this chapter I realized that it would perhaps require its own introduction and guide if one hoped to provide a complete sketch of it. Chapter 6, then, neither presents the background figures nor attempts to trace the shape of certain concepts, but rather aims to capture something of the essence of the "non-philosophical order" by locating it within contemporary philosophy generally, specifically in the domain of Continental philosophy, and its relation to post-Kantian philosophy specifically.

Chapter 1 provides a history of the development of Laruelle's non-philosophy with special attention to the relationship between science and philosophy in that development. There are various ways to present such a history, and elsewhere I have done so via a study of the variations of Laruelle's axioms, but owing to the focus of *Principles of Non-Philosophy*, understanding the relationship of science and philosophy is paramount.[5] In the remainder of the chapter I will discuss the purpose of *Principles of Non-Philosophy* and where it fits within Laruelle's development of non-philosophy generally, before turning to the explication of two key concepts ("the One" and "radical immanence") that one needs to have a grasp on in order to make sense of the rest of Laruelle's text as well as this guide. Finally, I provide a short overview of the organization of *Principles of Non-Philosophy* itself.

Chapter 2 focuses again on the question of how non-philosophy conceives of philosophy and science. The phenomenology of Edmund Husserl and the metamathematics of Kurt Gödel figure prominently. The work of these two figures is used by Laruelle to explain how he conceives of a "unified theory of philosophy and science," a concept that gets to the heart of non-philosophy's democratic spirit.

Chapter 3 explores the conception of the subject in non-philosophy. Here, again, the phenomenological tradition is of special importance and we contrast Laruelle's conception of the subject as a "force-(of)-thought" with the classic Cartesian "thinking thing" as it is taken up by Immanuel Kant and later Jean-Luc Marion and Michel Henry. Laruelle's conception of a unified theory is important in this chapter as well, though now it aims at a unified theory of the subject and the ego. Hence Laruelle's engagement here with psychoanalysis as the other great discourse of the subject in European philosophy. Ultimately, for Laruelle, the unified theory of the subject will be best understood as a force-(of)-thought rather than an entity or simple projection.

Chapter 4 examines the special causal logic of non-philosophy described as "determination-in-the-last-instance" or "unilateralization." Following Laruelle's own practice, we explicate this concept in dialogue with J.G. Fichte's *Wissenschaftslehre* or *Science of Knowledge*. Here a schematism of determination-in-the-last-instance is sketched out in relation to Laruelle's conception of the One, the (non-)One, and the non(-One). This provides for a formal understanding of determination-in-the-last-instance as well as of the conception of cloning that can often be mystifying to readers despite being of central importance in *Principles of Non-Philosophy*.

Chapter 5 turns to the method of dualysis and explores the way it functions. This is carried out by surveying three instances of dualysis: 1) Being and Alterity or Otherness (with reference to the Greek and Jewish shape of contemporary European philosophy); 2) reason and mythology (with reference to the notion of universality in philosophy); and 3) life and death (with reference to the concept of the "lived" in non-philosophy). With the survey of these instances of dualysis we also begin to place Laruelle in the context of contemporary European philosophy more generally, through discussions of Jacques Derrida, Gilles Deleuze, Max Horkheimer and Theodor Adorno, Alain Badiou, Michel Henry, and Ray Brassier.

As discussed above, Chapter 6 presents a reading of non-philosophy within the contemporary philosophical scene. While I accept that the distinction between analytic and Continental philosophy is largely artificial and intellectually untenable, the two terms are operative within academic philosophy and establish boundaries, however fuzzy, for certain concerns and concepts. Here we see how Laruelle takes up these concerns and concepts in a post-Continental form, before turning to look at some specific post-Kantian themes that are mutated and recast by non-philosophy.

1

Situating Principles of Non-Philosophy: *Introductory Concepts and First Names*

THE TASK OF PRINCIPLES OF NON-PHILOSOPHY

There is a peculiarity to the reception of Laruelle that is nevertheless common to any philosopher whose works are discovered late in his or her development. While Laruelle's non-philosophy has developed organically, it has also until very recently developed largely without any interaction with his Anglophone readers. Only now, nearly forty years after Laruelle began his project, are Anglophone readers beginning to look at his work. But each individual work now fits within a wider development not clearly seen by those readers. So while *Principles of Non-Philosophy* remains incredibly consistent with his earlier *Philosophies of Difference* (originally published in French in 1986 and in English translation by Rocco Gangle in 2010), and builds off the groundwork laid there, it would be a mistake to read *Principles of Non-Philosophy* as the final mature formulation of his work, much in the same way we cannot simply take Husserl's *Logical Investigations* or Badiou's *Theory of the Subject* as the end of their philosophical development.[1] *Principles of Non-Philosophy*, like the earlier important texts *Philosophies of Difference* and *Philosophy and Non-Philosophy* (originally published in French in 1989 and in English translation by Taylor Adkins in 2013), is not the final, achieved text of non-philosophy. But also like these earlier works, it is one of the central texts where the principles of non-philosophy are laid out, as the title suggests. And so for those interested in what non-philosophy can do it remains a vital text, one which this introduction and guide will show has contemporary philosophical relevance.

What was Laruelle's purpose in writing the text? First, it should be noted that Laruelle is very suspicious of the usual philosophical obsession with teleology or ends. The notion of the end or finality of things can be a form of harassment for human beings, always treating them as mere steps upon the way to something other than the human, as in anti-humanism, or as falling outside the so-called essence of the human and so not properly human at all, as in humanism. For Laruelle, thought guided by an assumed end is part of the harassing character of philosophy, for within this kind of thinking there is a demand from the side of philosophy that everything submit to this philosophically determined hierarchy of ends. So to ask the question of the purpose of non-philosophy opens up to all sorts of misunderstandings, as Laruelle himself warns, and unsurprisingly he resists spelling out such purposes straightforwardly so as to avoid philosophical re-appropriation. We can begin to address the question, however, by way of a *via negativa*, or saying what the ends are not. While Laruelle's work, especially as represented in the phase of his development he calls Philosophy II (which includes *Philosophies of Difference* and *Philosophy and Non-Philosophy*), does include a critique of philosophy, non-philosophy is not another discourse on the "end of philosophy." This has a double meaning, though it should be kept in mind that both are examples of metaphilosophy. Non-Philosophy is concerned neither with the "proper role" of philosophy, its end in the sense of its place in the disciplinary structures of a university education, nor with hastening the so-called "death of philosophy." Non-Philosophy is not an anti-philosophy, it is not concerned with destroying philosophy.

From here we can move on to a more positive discussion of what non-philosophy does aim to do. Consider first what Laruelle states as one of the positive aspects of non-philosophy:

> If philosophy has only been and only will be an opinion and a poorly thought out passion, then the question is of passing from its state of war and of competition, a state of exploitation of thought and as such of man, to its civil state, which we want to call human and democratic. This democratic humanization is one of the objectives – if there are any – of non-philosophy and perhaps even the only objective, if we decide to put the Real at the heart of man or man at the heart of the Real rather than one at the periphery of the other as philosophy itself does.[2]

In other words, the goal of non-philosophy, if we can call it a goal, is the creation of a *"new democratic order of thought"* that will disempower the hierarchical relation within philosophy and within the relationship of philosophy to other disciplines (what Laruelle calls "regional knowledges" or "knowings"). This is very different than talking about a complete disordering of the relationship between philosophy and other disciplines, and Laruelle will differentiate "order" from "domination." The reason this differentiation between order and domination works is because of the way in which Laruelle thinks of the relation between philosophy and the regional forms of knowledge or ways of knowing (i.e. particular forms of science, ethical ways of living, religious discourses, etc.). Non-Philosophy seeks to identify the identity or "essence" of philosophy and a regional knowledge; in this text the regional knowledge at play is science in its general meaning and so not a particular form of science (biology, physics, etc.). However, these identities are not sought so as to fit them within some wider hierarchy of ends, rather they are thought so as to be re-ordered "from the Real." We will return to this concept of the Real at greater length later in this chapter, but what it means in terms of the proposed "democracy-(of)-thought" is an opening up of lines of engagement between these forms of knowing.

While Laruelle himself does not make this suggestion, we could think of this democracy-(of)-thought as a form of interdisciplinary or transdisciplinary work. While these two terms have taken on a certain buzzword character, threatening to strip them of anything meaningful outside of something a researcher must pay lip service to in funding applications, they also arose out of a certain promise of mutual aid between disciplines that would help break new ground and foster new discoveries. Non-Philosophy offers resources for transdisciplinary work.[3] These resources are not made explicit by Laruelle himself but we can delineate a few principles that the reader may note as they read through the chapters "Introduction" and "The Problematic of Non-Philosophy": 1) The identity of a discipline or "regional knowledge" can be located. In simple terms, disciplines have distinct practices and approaches to whatever object of study they have taken up. 2) These distinct practices are not sufficient in themselves to the practice of thought in general. Take the example of a living organism (though to call something "a living organism" is rife with philosophical problems and is already a decision, but let us bracket that for the moment). While a biologist may tell us about the chemical composition of a living organism, a poet may be able to give meaning to the life of that organism, and a philosopher may provide the conditions for the possibility of knowing that organism, none of these thinks the organism as complete and in–itself. Such was the thinking that in part motivated Husserl's investigations and development of the phenomenological method in an attempt to find some apodictic or certain knowledge. But Husserl did not investigate in the same depth the way in which philosophy itself may be like that living organism. Laruelle's claim then is similar to Husserl but begins to apply this notion of the incomplete knowledge of something like a living organism to philosophy itself. More than that, he claims that no form of knowledge is sufficient to think its own identity completely, metaphilosophy or metascience will always necessarily be incomplete (Laruelle claims this following Kurt Gödel, discussed in the following chapter). 3) This incompleteness, however, does not mean that science needs philosophy, or philosophy needs science. Disciplines are able to make themselves consistent within their own practices and so have autonomy, albeit an autonomy that is relative. 4) This relative autonomy is not relative to a single discipline, but to the Real. Without yet unpacking what the concept of the Real signifies, we could translate this into simpler terms by saying that the relative autonomy of disciplines is always relative to something "outside" the totality of those disciplines. From Laruelle's perspective this seeming "outside" would have to recognize the basis of these knowings, rooted as they are in human existence and so not outside in any real sense but rather separate from these forms of knowledge. There is a call in non-philosophy to a defense of this human against the domination of the human by authoritarian forms of knowledge, though not as explicitly within *Principles of Non-Philosophy* as elsewhere.[4]

Laruelle opens himself up here to charges of anthropocentrism and it is true that until his most recent work, which has seen some attempts to think through the identity of the "animal," there has been an exclusive focus on the human.[5] However, from Laruelle's perspective, such a focus is justified because of philosophy's harassment and debasing of the human. A harassment and debasing present not just in Nietzschean calls to overcome humanity, but in the various humanisms that never think the lived identity of a human being, instead attempting to think the human in relation to some transcendental attribute that erases that lived reality, or what Laruelle will call the radical immanence of the human. To state this accurately from a non-philosophical perspective I have to use a strange formulation that I will then explain. All forms of knowing, whether they be philosophical or scientific, are manifested from a lived human. In normal, idiomatic speech I would be expected to add some modifier like "lived human experience" or "lived human reality," however that is precisely the philosophical vision Laruelle is trying to avoid, a philosophical vision that can only think the human by way of some relational and transcendental attribute (experience or reality in this case) rather than thinking, as non-philosophy aims to, the radical identity of the human. Science and philosophy are manifest from the human. Or, in the technical language of non-philosophy, the identities or essences of philosophy and science are unilaterally related to the radical immanence of the human. At this stage we may come to a better understanding of this goal of non-philosophy if we turn to Laruelle's development of the philosophy/science relationship throughout his work. As we will see, this relationship is at the heart of the non-philosophical project.

10

HISTORY OF NON-PHILOSOPHY AS THE HISTORY OF THE CONJUGATION OF PHILOSOPHY AND SCIENCE

As works by Laruelle begin to be translated into English, the Anglophone reader faces the challenge both of understanding the individual text and of placing that text within the development of non-philosophy. Laruelle provides a short history of non-philosophy in "The Problematic of Non-Philosophy" chapter of *Principles of Non-Philosophy*. He has also separated out five distinct phases in his development, which he labels Philosophy I–V. Of course, *Principles of Non-Philosophy* is situated in that history and finds its place in what he calls Philosophy III. While there is a major difference between Philosophy I and Philosophy II (namely the move from writing purely philosophical texts to the development of non-philosophy), and there is a great difference between Philosophy II and Philosophy III (which is explained in *Principles of Non-Philosophy* as the complete dismantling of any dominating hierarchy), all of the developments from Philosophy III to V have been far subtler. *Principles of Non-Philosophy* really does function remarkably as a model of the general practice and form of non-philosophy from its writing onward. Elsewhere I have provided a different explanation of this history, focusing on the axioms which organize each phase, but we can also understand the history of non-philosophy as the history of the continuous attempt to conjugate philosophy and science.[6]

The term "non-philosophy" (which I put in scare quotes when referring to those conceptions of non-philosophy that are different from Laruelle's) is of course not an original coinage by Laruelle. He himself recognizes the fact of a philosophical history and elaboration of a very different kind of non-philosophy. In his "Introduction" he traces this history, beginning in the eighteenth century with Kant and those who came after him as situating a "non-philosophical" Other that shows the limits and abilities of philosophy itself. But this continues up to contemporary French philosophy, where we can find Merleau-Ponty delimitating philosophy in a similar Kantian way and Deleuze reflecting on the need for a "nonphilosophy" in order to grasp the plane of immanence at the heart of philosophical inquiry. But for Laruelle what distinguishes this history of "non-philosophy" from the project he is pursuing is that the history of these "nonphilosophies" are *philosophical* "nonphilosophies" (we can symbolize this difference by leaving out the hyphen, symbolizing the ways in which they are outside of the philosophical tradition in a way that non-philosophy, in Laruelle's sense, is not). In other words, philosophy always appeals to something outside of philosophy in order to complete it, but philosophy itself remains untouched by this "nonphilosophy." Each of these philosophical "nonphilosophies" presents materials from other disciplines, like art, the natural and social sciences, political practice, cultural production, and more. As Laruelle says,

> Each philosophy defines then a non-philosophical margin that it tolerates, circumscribes, reappropriates, or which it *uses* in order to expropriate itself: as beyond or other to philosophical mastery. So its concern is with a 'non' whose content and means of action are ontic or empirical, ontological in the best cases, but whose reach is limited by this mastery.[7]

These materials and disciplines are not properly philosophical but they are *tolerated* in some sense by philosophy proper and not without philosophical reason. Philosophy treats these materials and disciplines in the same way that the capitalist treats the worker: philosophy expropriates value from the labor of these materials and disciplines in order ultimately to provide support for the very system that is expropriating that value. Non-Philosophy, in Laruelle's sense, is no longer taken as something under philosophy, but is now an autonomous discipline separate from philosophy, completely useless for philosophy proper, and useless precisely in taking up the same posture as science has.

Remember that following the disempowering of the usual philosophical hierarchy of philosophy and science, to take up the posture of science is not to proclaim the end of philosophy. Laruelle goes to great lengths to make clear that "non-philosophy" does not designate some outside of philosophy, "an external-internal condition of philosophical activity," nor an "anti-philosophy" that would constitute an attempt to end philosophy altogether.[8] It is here, in navigating the pure affirmation or pure negation of philosophy, that non-philosophy begins to act like a science. The "non-" of non-philosophy takes its cue from, or models itself on, the sciences, in particular non-Euclidean geometry. Non-Euclidean geometry does not replace Euclidean geometry, it is not an "anti-Euclidean" form of geometry, but instead has a twofold relationship with standard Euclidean geometry. First, it began by changing the axioms by which Euclidean geometry works. Euclid's geometry is based on five postulates or axioms and non-Euclidean geometry is constituted by one of these axioms being suspended. This axiom, called the parallel postulate, claimed that all parallel lines would extend in space at an equal distance without ever meeting or diverging from that distance. By setting this axiom aside a different foundation for mathematical works was established which, when developed, was shown to be able to work with problems that Euclidean geometry could not. In standard Euclidean geometry the parallel postulate maintains that one and only one line can be drawn through any point not on a given line parallel to the given line in a plane. In short, this meant that lines would be parallel if the sum of their angles added up to 180 degrees. What non-Euclidean geometry was able to do by suspending this axiom and negating it in various ways was open up the understanding of space to include relativity. In overly simple terms, more than one line or no line at all could be drawn through a single point depending on whether the geometry is dealing with a hyperbolic or elliptic plane which the line sits upon.

Again, this did not replace Euclidean geometry. That sort of vision of a single disciplinary discourse on the universe given to us by peddlers of popular science (referring to those scientists who offer a kind of pop philosophy with regard to the "big questions") rarely matches up with actual scientific research programs. In fact not only does non-Euclidean geometry not replace standard Euclidean geometry, it actually allowed for a renewed understanding of the latter and new variations of its standard operations. In the same way non-philosophy aims to be able to provide a new framework that will allow for traditional philosophical problems to be approached in new ways.

Principles of Non-Philosophy is an extended attempt to translate the mature practice of non-philosophy into a formal system by addressing the traditional philosophical problem of epistemology. We can see that formal system at play in one of the clearly stated purposes behind *Principles of Non-Philosophy*, which is to bring together philosophy and science in a wider democracy-(of)-thought. If "order" is to be opposed to domination in any meaningful sense, it can only come through this democratization of philosophy and science and any other form of regional knowing. With regard to philosophy this happens, for Laruelle, through the *"non-philosophical translation of philosophies."*[9] This non-philosophical translation disempowers philosophy with regard to its assumed sufficiency. One major aspect of that translation is the conjugation or collision of two terms or objects. In non-philosophy these objects are either various forms of philosophy or philosophy and some other regional knowledge.

This conjugation has been present throughout Laruelle's work and when looking through his texts you can always see an attempt to think two styles of thought together. With regard to different philosophies this is present most obviously in one of his other major works that has been translated into English, *Philosophies of Difference*. In this text Laruelle attempts to think together Heidegger and Nietzsche and Derrida and Deleuze in order to uncover the invariant form of philosophy as present in the philosophies of difference. In his 2010 *Philosophie non-standard* which belongs to his most recent phase of Philosophy V, Laruelle conceived of the project of non-philosophy as a kind of collision. He explains this idea of non-philosophy as creating a conjugation of two philosophies in a 2012 interview, saying:

I have always used two philosophies at the same time. Heidegger and Nietzsche, then Derrida and Deleuze. So it is always a matter of how to eventually combine several philosophies. [...] I had the feeling that in order to completely change the concept of philosophy, two philosophies were always necessary, as if each of the philosophers represented half of philosophy, basically, which I felt to be the non-completeness of a particular philosophy; this problem would have to be resolved each time by the combination of two philosophers. I have followed this way of doing things, a little bit in spite of myself, always combining two philosophies as if each of them was lacking what the other had. You could think that this is a dialectical relation. But in fact that was not that at all, because it was, each time, two philosophies and not one philosophy and the entire history of philosophy in addition. Thus, I am part of a conjugation, I like this term a lot, of philosophies which replaced the missing concept. What was missing was the One, the One-in-One.[10]

Setting aside for now the concept of the One-in-One, which we touch on in Chapter 4, what does this image of the collider and the conjugation of philosophy tell us about non-philosophy? Consider how Laruelle opens the book: "One philosopher does not succeed another without claiming to succeed philosophy itself as a whole. That is how, with knowing it, they renew the original or grounding philosophical gesture. As for non-philosophy: which philosophy does it succeed? [...] Non-Philosophy only claims to succeed the faith and authority of philosophy."[11] The goal of non-philosophy is not to destroy the philosophy indexed by this or that name – so Nietzsche, Heidegger, Derrida, and Deleuze are safe from non-philosophical harm or usurpation – but to enlarge these philosophies by bringing them together with another style of philosophy to produce something in the space left open there.

So does this conjugation of two different philosophies match what we find in *Principles of Non-Philosophy*? No, instead we find a more general conjugation. We do find a simpler dualism of philosophy (including epistemology and specifically phenomenology, Descartes being included as a part of this tradition, following the studies of Marion) and science. This attempt to think philosophy and science in Laruelle's oeuvre is not particular to *Principles of Non-Philosophy*, even if the latter was the most developed account prior to his very recent work. In the preface Laruelle states that *Principles of Non-Philosophy* is a preliminary work to another that is to come. This future work, which he refers to as "Science première," would be the "realization of non-philosophy in traditional and scientific material." A work under this title was never published, but arguably his 2010 *Philosophie non-standard. Générique, quantique, philo-fiction* constitutes just such a volume. In fact this text originally bore the working title *Nouveaux principes de la non-philosophie* or *New Principles of Non-Philosophy*. In *Philosophie non-standard*, non-philosophy is said to be "accomplished" in a form bringing together the standard practice of philosophy with the contemporary scientific practice of research in quantum mechanics. This work is important in part because we can see there the conjugation model at its most developed. Here Laruelle takes up a specific scientific practice alongside the practice of philosophy in order to think the concepts within that scientific practice as already in some sense doing philosophical work. To use an image other than conjugation we have already touched on, *Philosophie non-standard* gives us the image of the particle collider and the idea of bringing together two different particles (the practice of philosophical theory and the practice of the science of quantum mechanics) in order to develop a new, better understanding of the "stuff" they are made of.

But this work emerges out of decades of research in thinking through the practices of both philosophy and the sciences. So one way we can trace the history of non-philosophy's development is to follow the different ways philosophy and science have been brought together. Prior to *Principles of Non-Philosophy*, in books such as *Philosophies of Difference* and *Philosophy and Non-Philosophy*, Laruelle primarily thought of the relationship between philosophy and science along the lines of a "science of philosophy." What this meant in practice was a submission of philosophy to science. This wasn't a submission of philosophy to any particular science, however, it was not a sociological analysis of philosophy or a mathematical account (whatever these might look like and whatever their value might be), but instead was a submission of philosophy to the general posture of science. In this period of non-philosophy's development philosophy was investigated for the identity that it itself could not find. This science of philosophy allowed Laruelle to locate the Philosophical Decision as the fundamental guiding structure for all philosophical practice.[12] However, while Laruelle retains a great deal from his science of philosophy (including both the discovery of Philosophical Decision and the posture of science), he also came to see the relation of philosophy to science as merely a reversal of the usual hierarchy proposed by philosophy. This normal philosophical hierarchy sees science subordinated and dominated by philosophy, seeing itself as providing the necessary "thought" for science that science cannot provide for itself. In these earlier texts he merely reversed this hierarchy, dominating philosophy with the general image of science.

With *Principles of Non-Philosophy* this hierarchy is dismantled completely in favor of the "minimal order" mentioned already. This minimal order refers again to the ordering of philosophy and science. Now, instead of one relating to the other directly, the order is carried out by making them both relatively autonomous to one another in relation to the radical autonomy of the Real. This is an important move as it contains within it the logic of determination-in-the-last-instance (abbreviated as DLI), which will be discussed in Chapter 4, so if the reader is able to follow the move here they will be better positioned to understand the general concept of DLI. First, it is important to note that we have three terms: philosophy, science, and the Real. These terms share something in common in the description, they are all referred to in relation to autonomy. That philosophy and science have autonomy means that they are able to determine their own identity, that they have practices which are theirs and which can be changed and directed from within the discipline itself. In short, these disciplines have agency of their own accord. However, to say that they have *relative* autonomy means that this self-direction happens within some wider relation to something that determines these terms at a more general level. Instead of this determination coming from another form of knowledge, that is, instead of another form of knowledge dominating the other, this wider relation is to the Real. We will explain more fully this concept of the Real (or the One, these terms are equivalent in Laruelle to the point that he often refers to them as "the real-One") shortly, but here one only need to see that the Real has *radical* autonomy. This means that, while the Real provides a minimal determination or conditions of possibility for philosophy and science, the Real is not effected by these disciplines. This kind of causality is referred to both as DLI and unilateral. What it means practically is that there is a certain kind of equality between philosophy and science, because both are relative to the Real. But this relativity means that the equality is not what Laruelle refers to as a "unitary levelling" or "anarchizing multiplicity."[13] In other words, while this relative autonomy destroys the strong hierarchical vision of the relationship between philosophy and science, it does not create a space of pure chaos between the disciplines. It is able to recognize their identity, which comes down to recognizing what both philosophy and science *do* and allowing for these different kinds of actions to retain their relative value.

So, to return our focus to the development of the relationship between philosophy and science in non-philosophy and to sum it up, we can see that Laruelle begins in his earliest work by submitting philosophy to science, which allows for an image of science to dominate over philosophy. This led him to the discovery of philosophy's fundamental essence, Philosophical Decision, as well as the value of the scientific posture, but it was suspect and prone to error because it simply inverted the *philosophical* hierarchy of philosophy and science. Whereas, in Philosophy III, and its mature formulation with *Principles of Non-Philosophy*, this hierarchy is dismantled in favor of a democracy-(of)-thought, which is built out of the causality of DLI. This democracy-(of)-thought is more specifically a development of what Laruelle calls a unified theory of philosophy and science, but even though this unified theory is clearly at play, we see the conjugation method working very differently than in *Philosophies of Difference* or his later *Anti-Badiou* (which is arguably an attempt to think Badiou's philosophy and Laruelle's philosophy together as two unified philosophies). Instead what we find in *Principles of Non-Philosophy* is a more abstract or formal development of this method where Laruelle steps back and empties out the specific content indexed by these philosophers' names in order to understand the form of philosophy, science, and non-philosophy. What marks out *Principles of Non-Philosophy* as a major text in Laruelle's development of non-philosophy is that he does not here attempt to bring together two philosophers, but instead makes a great leap forward and attempts to think together philosophy *as such* with science *as such*. This becomes important as later works like *Ethique de l'Etranger* (*Ethics of the Stranger* or *Stranger Ethics*, originally published in 2000) and *Future Christ* (originally published in 2002 and in English translation in 2010) move away from the bringing together of philosopher X and philosopher Y and instead try to bring together philosophy and ethics as such or philosophy and religion as such.

THE THREE DISCOVERIES OF NON-PHILOSOPHY

In the chapters ahead the reader will be introduced to a number of important methodological concepts and theoretical positions advanced by Laruelle. However, there are a number of equally important foundational concepts that Laruelle lays out in his opening chapter, "The Problematic of Non-Philosophy." These concepts, or "first names" as Laruelle prefers to call them, are important to keep in mind as the reader moves through the rest of the text, for they are the most general and abstract formulations that structure every other form of thought in the text. The reason he calls them "names" instead of concepts or terms owes to the way in which names lack sufficiency and always suggest a kind of fictive element that is nonetheless real. For the sake of familiarity and in a kind of act of translation, I will refer to these as concepts, but the reader should understand that a concept is, in this book, a kind of "name" in the sense outlined above. Depending on the reader's own knowledge base, some of these concepts will have an air of familiarity, others will seem utterly foreign. This owes to the incredible richness and variety of what might traditionally be called Laruelle's sources, but which in his work become simply materials or influences in the sense one might mean when discussing a musician or artist. That is, when reading his texts, *Principles of Non-Philosophy* included, a reader steeped in the history of French and German philosophy will begin to notice and pick out a number concepts clearly derived from elsewhere, but the function and shape of which is often, if not always, transformed or recast by Laruelle.

Starting with the section entitled "The three discoveries which ground non-philosophy" Laruelle presents a truncated summary of a number of the concepts that he will be developing throughout *Principles of Non-Philosophy*. It is worth keeping these three discoveries in mind as the book ultimately revolves around their explication. Summarizing them he writes:

> It is not the question of the end and the ends of philosophy, but *that of a non-philosophical discovery that we would not yet have made and which would change the face of philosophy*. This discovery, probably, cannot be made without the renunciation of the question of its death, a question which is moreover that of its sufficiency to be adequate to the Real, the real of death. It comprises three facets:
>
> - The essence of the One as radical immanence or vision-in-One, correctly understood, is the first discovery; that of the conditions that must be reaized in order that immanence can be effectively "radical"; or, again, the concept of Given-without-givenness.
> - The causality of the real-One as determination-in-the-last-instance, which is first made concrete on the occasion of the organon that is the force-(of)-thought.
> - The form of thought adequate to the radical autonomy of the One, the form of an organon which works through hypothesis or axiomatic yet "real" decision rather than through a thesis or philosophical decision; as such the abandonment of the thematic of "thought" in lieu of an organon of thought, and the distinction between the two absolutely heterogeneous concepts of decision.[14]

While couched here in highly technical language, the promise of Laruelle's book is that he will unpack these concentrated statements. However, for the sake of getting a grasp on them immediately here, we can group them according to where they would fit within a standard philosophical discourse separated into ontology, epistemology, and metaphilosophy. We will also unpack them in relation to how Laruelle sees philosophers and their philosophies distinguishing themselves from one another. For Laruelle, "The philosophers distinguish between themselves by *a system of diversely measured mixtures of immanence and transcendence*, by these infinitely varied twists and interlacings."[15] So we will relate these facets of non-philosophy to the general concepts of immanence and transcendence in so far as they play out in Laruelle's project.

As regards the first statement, the discovery of the radical immanence of the One, this may be mapped onto standard philosophical discourse on ontology. Ontology, or the study of Being qua Being, has tended to deal in convertibility, meaning that it attempts to explain Being through reference to something else which it can be converted with, like logic or structure (*logos*). The study of ontology takes different forms in the two main Western philosophical cultures, which tend to be called Continental and analytic despite clear problems with both the names and the thematic of their division. During the twentieth-century, ontology has tended to be understood within the Continental mainstream in terms broadly set by Martin Heidegger's philosophy. Heidegger's philosophy made bold demands of philosophers. First, he challenged them to take up the true task of thinking, which in his writing tarries close to a kind of mystical demand seemingly against the culture of science, while nevertheless demanding this task of thinking not be rooted in religion either. If we were to summarize Heidegger's war cry against modern culture it would be "we do not know yet what thinking is (because we have forgotten what the Greeks knew)." So Heidegger demanded that we think, and what was paramount to be thought was Being qua Being, what always remains unthought and yet seems to hold together our everyday speech. Even considering that war cry, the question of being sticks out there for it claims that we do not yet know what thinking *is*. Heidegger developed his own reading of the history of philosophy, which has been very influential on the philosophers who came after him. In that history the question of Being was raised by the ancient Greek philosophers but was forgotten as later philosophers answered the question by making it a question of individual beings and not Being qua Being. Individual beings refer to things like the book you are holding your hand. If you were to ask yourself, "What is the being of this book?" you may naturally begin to answer by breaking down the parts of the book. And the parts may take on very different aspects, which may be material or social or any number of other things. So you may want to say that the book is bound printed matter, or something created to be marketed and sold, or just atoms arranged in a pattern, or whatever. Yet, for Heidegger, when you answer the question of Being in this way you are actually *forgetting Being*. Because none of these answers actually address the Being of the book, but instead refer to other individual beings, be they atoms, or social systems, or everyday materials like paper and glue. For each of those individual beings the book is reduced to, the question of their Being remains. What does it mean to be an atom that can make up something that is not just an atom? What does it mean to be a social system that can contain things like books which are not, as paper or atoms, a social system? And so on.

This difference between individual beings and Being is referred to by

Heidegger as "Ontological Difference" and Laruelle addresses this structure of Heidegger's philosophy in *Philosophies of Difference*. Ultimately, in his own attempt to create a non-philosophy, Laruelle will seek to generalize Heidegger's ontological difference rather than simply negate it. If what Heidegger does is think Being qua Being then what would it mean to generalize this? The question arises because the question of Being in Heidegger already seems to be general. It is a question about what all individual beings share in so far as they *are* or have being. However, for Laruelle this ends up being a purely philosophical move, meaning that it confuses its own thought with the Real. In other words, Being ends up as another form of transcendence imposed upon the figure of the Human thereby covering over the radical identity or immanence of the Human. Instead of thinking from this radical immanence we do the same thing that Heidegger claims philosophers have done when thinking about Being. That is, we took something we were supposed to be thinking, in this case the Human, and we explain it by reference to something other than the Human. Laruelle is not here making a demand for some mystical experience of wholeness or a rejection of the powers found in science where we may understand something *in part* by breaking it down. The point for Laruelle is that even when we break something down, whether it be philosophically or scientifically, there is still an identity that is radical for that thing. So breaking down this book into its atomic structure reveals an identity of an atomic structure. Thus instead of thinking identity in terms of Being or Difference or under any other ontological structure, Laruelle moves to generalize by becoming even more abstract. This is why he chooses "the One" as the name for identity and radical immanence.

The term "the One," which is again an equivalent for his term "the Real," is chosen because it is more abstract than Being. Therefore, to understand the meaning of the term "the One" we first have to differentiate it from the other philosophical depictions of the One. In this chapter laying out non-philosophy's problematic Laruelle quickly differentiates the One from all other philosophical forms of the One ("Parmenides' 'spherical' One-Being, Heraclitus' One-All, Plotinus' One-in-procession-conversion, Spinoza's Unity-God of substances and attributes, Fichte's I = I, Wittgenstein's 'Internal Relation' and its immanence, etc.")[16] by denying the convertibility of the One with anything other than the One itself. Sometimes he will speak about this radical identity of the One by writing it as "One-in-One," meaning that the One is only related, from its perspective, to itself. It is important then that the One, while abstract, is not the numerical 1. The One is simply a symbol of identity or a translation of the lived reality of radical immanence without any predicates or transcendent modifiers added to it. This is precisely what Laruelle means when he claims that non-philosophy is the discovery of the radical immanence of the One. This discovery arises out of the bringing together of philosophical theory with an image of scientific practice, which Laruelle explores in more depth in "'First Science' as Unified Theory of Science and Philosophy: Or, Democracy within Thought" and which is the focus of Chapter 2 of this text.

ABSOLUTE AND RADICAL IMMANENCE: DELEUZE AND HENRY

The figure of immanence has taken an increasingly central position in European thought, but for readers new to philosophy it can appear mystifying – so adding the modifier "radical" to an already mystifying concept may be even more mystifying. The centrality of immanence for contemporary philosophy perhaps owes in part to the influence of Gilles Deleuze, who most clearly lays out his understanding of immanence as "the plane of immanence" in his book *What Is Philosophy?*, co-written with Félix Guattari. There he thinks of the history of philosophy as the history of the institution of the plane of immanence of a One-All produced largely from his interpretation of Spinoza.[17] Here immanence is a name for the absolute character of Nature and Mind, picking up again the Spinozist theme of God (or Substance) having two attributes we know (extension and thought). In other words, there is something going on in philosophies concerned with immanence that rejects any reality to notions of transcendence. Both immanence and transcendence are spatial terms. So when Deleuze writes about immanence he is referring ultimately to the idea that all the relations and becomings of any entity (a person, a tree, a text, and so on) take place on the same level of reality. There is no escaping from what is, no Platonic world of forms where the Truth resides, and no God in the sky who has another reality prepared behind this world. Every truth, every joy, every beautiful thing that exists comes from the same plane of reality, the One-All. Transcendence is ultimately, for Deleuze and those who follow him, simply an illusion or a ruse of power, stories that people tell other people in order to rule over them.

Laruelle is clearly influenced by Deleuze's thinking on immanence, however he claims that Deleuze makes a mistake in thinking immanence as "absolute": immanence in Deleuze's philosophy comes to function in the same way Deleuze claims transcendence does in other philosophies and in theology or religious thought. Immanence is taken as a Spinozist One-All operating as a quasi-thing above the human, and so against Deleuze's best hopes for what immanence would be, in his philosophy immanence is something that an entity relates to. This creates a confusion between "absolute immanence" and an "absolute transcendence," because ultimately transcendence refers to a relation as well, a relation between two "things," one above the other in terms of their reality or in terms of how intensive their existence is.

Laruelle usually employs the modifier "radical" to refer to his own conception of immanence, but his use of the term owes much to the work of Michel Henry. The importance of Henry's work for Laruelle cannot be understated and one can see it running through his early works up through the present. That influence is perhaps most clear, if passed over in relative silence, in *Principles of Non-Philosophy*, but Laruelle discusses it more explicitly in his *Introduction to Non-Marxism*, where Henry's humanist reading of Marx is brought together with the anti-humanism of Louis Althusser's reading. But it is in *Struggle and Utopia at the End Times of Philosophy*, where he devotes a chapter to discussing the "Left and Right of Non-Philosophy," that Laruelle locates Henry's "radical phenomenology" as a forerunner to his own non-philosophy, albeit from a rightist perspective.[18] This nomination of Henry as representing the "right-wing of non-philosophy" owes to Henry's attempt to conserve philosophy's self-sufficiency in being able to philosophize science, and to his own conservative position on the philosophical scene in France as an explicitly Catholic phenomenologist seemingly terrified of the ways in which technology and non-Christian forms of thinking about life threaten to lead to a new barbarism. Theological themes are found in Henry's earliest major work, *The Essence of Manifestation*, through an engagement with the Christian medieval theologian and mystic Meister Eckhart, but his conservative stance towards technology resulted in his later work taking an even more explicit theological turn as an attempt to recover what he saw as the radical philosophy of life found in Christianity.[19]

However, these conservative aspects of Henry's thought are not taken up at all by Laruelle, whose own political views are clearly of a more left-wing persuasion, if also harboring some concerns over the ways in which any political use of theory or technology may end up as a form of domination over the lives of human beings they are supposed to improve. What is important for Laruelle in Henry's philosophy is his critique of the ontological monism of philosophy which requires a split conception of being (being as such and consciousness of being) and his attempt to overcome that ontological monism by thinking Being according to radical immanence. For Henry the traditional phenomenology of Husserl and Heidegger posits a fundamental ontological monism where "There is no difference between the philosophy of consciousness and the philosophy of Being."[20] This would seem to imply that there is no separation between consciousness of Being and Being in itself, and yet such an ontology requires a split between consciousness and Being in its understanding of the manifestation of Being. For in the moment of a phenomenologist thinking or becoming conscious of her own Being, she has to "step back" or "elevate" herself from her immediacy such that the manifestation of Being is not Being itself but consciousness of Being. As Henry explains:

> *Consciousness signifies the essence of manifestation interpreted according to the fundamental ontological presuppositions of monism.* For this reason, because it identifies itself with the process of self-splitting and of the separation of the self from Being, consciousness is always presented in its task and in its becoming as an act of *separating itself from Being, of elevating itself above it, of steeping back* in relation to it, *of opposing itself* to it. Thus, the rise of consciousness appears in its contemporaneity, together with the unfolding of a distance, with the accomplishment of a division, of a separation, of an opposition to itself. Moreover, it is precisely division, separation, opposition which were *the conditions of phenomenality in ontological monism.*[21]

This "phenomenality" invoked by Henry refers to the appearing of Being as such, but such an understanding of Being is fundamentally split between consciousness and a pre-conscious immediacy that results in something termed "phenomenological distance." Such distance is not the same thing as the distance between your eye and the page you are reading these words on – phenomenological distance is not measurable distance, but the very distance necessary for things to appear as distinct from the horizon of other things. That is, phenomenological distance is, for Henry, a kind of naming of the "world, understood in its pure world-ness,"[22] the world being, as it is in part for Laruelle, the very shape and space in which things may come to appear, but which also shapes the way in which those things appear. For ultimately, this phenomenological distance is what allows for the split in the ontologically monist conception of Being. Being may get away from itself through consciousness of Being, it may become Being-in-itself (immediate) or Being-for-itself (at a distance from, mediated or represented to itself). Thus, on Henry's reading, all attempts by ontological monists to understand what manifestation is (Being-for-itself or the consciousness of Being) have begun by positing Being outside itself such that, "In this Being-outside-itself, the Being-in-itself becomes clear, *it alienates itself and in this alienation, are realized the very conditions of its manifestation. Alienation is the essence of manifestation.*"[23]

Henry could not be clearer about the stakes of changing the way in which Being is thought. The promise of phenomenology was a return to the things themselves, a return to thinking the thing as it is in-itself rather than as distorted through the lenses of theories confusing themselves for the object. Yet, on Henry's reading, Husserlian and Heideggerian phenomenology ends up giving us a vision of Being that projects its own methodological structures and presuppositions into Being and consciousness of Being, leading to an alienation within thought that, as he makes clear in his reading of Marx, is deadly and life sapping like the more explicitly material form of alienation. Such an experience of alienation is occasioned by thinking according to phenomenological distance, that is by thinking according to the World as horizon. What Henry's radical phenomenology aims at is a way of thinking that would avoid the split monism of classical phenomenology, and of post-Kantian critical philosophy generally, and instead truly think the thing-in-itself according to itself. That is, Henry's project requires that he finds a way to think without recourse to phenomenological distance and so requires that he think from a position of radical immanence.

Laruelle's own work owes much to the way in which Henry unpacks the standard interplay of transcendence (the essence of phenomenological distance, according to Henry and Laruelle) and immanence in *The Essence of Manifestation*.[24] This interplay is another version of the split within ontological monism and inscribes within itself an impossibility of ever thinking immanence since it can only be thought in relation to transcendence, that is, at a distance to immanence, meaning only ever as already transcendent to immanence. What Henry then aims to do is think immanence as immanence, without relation to transcendence at all, a process he comes to name auto-affection and unpack over the course of his career. This thinking of the auto-affection of Being allows for a thinking of Being without splitting it, such that Henry may claim against the alienation present in ontological monism: "Essence is the essence of manifestation."[25] That is, by thinking from this sort of immanence he may finally think the essence of manifestation as itself, as immanence. This conception of immanence is ultimately a conception of immediacy in a technical sense: "Where there is no transcendence, there is neither horizon nor world."[26] In other words, Henry's sense of immanence is radically non-worldly, and this is taken up by Laruelle as a new conception of essence or identity. The immanence or immediacy of a thing is its uni-lateral determination or constitution, meaning that it does not dissolve itself and is not dissolved by something else into the World of mediation.[27]

Laruelle's conception of immanence as "radical" retains from Deleuze's Spinozist One-All a sense that this immanence is real, i.e. is not simply a concept or a construction of philosophy, but also retains from Henry's philosophy the idea that immanence is manifest as entities without any distance between those entities and some horizon of an "All."[28] Immanence is not a thing which another thing, like a person, relates to; rather, radical immanence refers to the very manifestation of that person without any difference existing between that manifestation and the person. This is what is meant by the idea of the "Given-without-givenness." Of course, again owing to the style of the book playing largely off the phenomenological tradition, this concept is derived from phenomenology and then mutated. What Laruelle is drawing attention to with this concept is an identity (radical immanence) of whatever appears (a given) without any transcendent predicate determining it. So the given only relates to itself, not to some transcendent notion of givenness, which in so far as it exists only does so because of the given. The relation between the given and givenness is, again, unilateral; that is, the givenness of a thing is dependent upon something actually being given.

This allows us to move to the second statement regarding the causality of the real-One, which clearly maps onto the standard philosophical investigation of causality and philosophies of action. The question it answers is: how do we understand the relationship between things? Of particular interest for Laruelle, this will be the question of the relationship between the Real and thought (thought being equally philosophy and science). And since it concerns a relation of this sort it opens up again the question of transcendence. Following Henry, this question of transcendence has to do ultimately with the interior relationship of the subject or ego. So this statement about causality carries another with it, that of the question of "an organon," or the question of what carries out this determination, which Laruelle he calls the force-(of)-thought. This is then a question moving from causality to subjectivity, which will be the focus of the chapter entitled "Unified or 'Non-Cartesian' Theory of the Subject: Duality of the Ego and the Subject" and is addressed in Chapter 3 of this text. This theory of the subject opens up to the question of what an identity is when seen from the perspective of radical immanence. The reason this is a question is because our normal ways of thinking about identity require us to appeal to something outside of the thing-in-itself – whether that be language in general or a specific predicate, there is an appeal to something transcendent to that thing-in-itself. Radical immanence does not negate transcendence, but discovers its identity as rooted in immanence and thus relative instead of absolute. Again the logic of DLI is paramount here. Transcendence has an identity for non-philosophy which is uncovered by DLI. For, from the perspective of philosophy there is something transcendent to it, namely the immanence of the real-One. Laruelle makes of this an axiom: "If immanence is radical, transcendence is autonomous and consistent and cannot be denied."[29] What does Laruelle mean by this? Simply, it is the logic of DLI at play, where from the perspective of one of the terms (radical immanence) there is only radical immanence, everything arises as determined by this radical immanence. This includes things taken as transcendent, for they will manifest radical immanence as well and as such they have an identity and a consistency that cannot simply be waived away without falling into error. This will be explored in more depth in the chapter "Determination-in-the-Last-Instance: Transcendental Theorem of the Force-(of)-Thought" as well as in Chapter 4 of this text.

The final statement can be mapped onto the standard philosophical investigation of method, both in epistemology, which asks the question "how do we know?," and in metaphilosophy, which asks "what is philosophy?" This is the focus of the longest chapter of *Principles of Non-Philosophy*, entitled "The Constitution of the Non-Philosophical Order." In many ways the reader should already have a sense of what this looks like, as the methodology has been discussed throughout this chapter. The order referred to is the discovery of a new way of ordering philosophy and science discussed earlier, as well as a way of ordering the relation of (radical) immanence and (relative) transcendence. These unified dualities or forms of knowing determined-in-the-last-instance are the path to undoing the Principle of Sufficient Philosophy (philosophy's faith in itself before the Real) before the radically lived Human.

2

On a Democracy Within Thought: Science and Philosophy as Citizens

There is a fundamental confusion in the contemporary everyday approach to the sciences. I will call this a double relation, the form of which will be familiar from Laruelle's own use and which refers in part to the way that the relation itself is not simple but has two, seemingly contradictory, aspects that constitute it.

On the one hand then, we are constantly bombarded with news stories that express fear at the progress of science. Perhaps these stories are simply examples of fear-mongering by the media, but what is interesting is the way in which this fear-mongering is presented as a kind of skepticism towards science and the challenges that its new discoveries bring. These stories are usually related to some specific discovery, for example at the time of Laruelle's writing *Principles of Non-Philosophy* there was massive public anxiety over the recent cloning of a sheep named Dolly and what the possibility of cloning would mean for the human species bio-politically. Here the concern is still not with science proper, but with the way science can appear to have a life of its own independent of any kind of popular will, especially under the regime of capitalist techno-science.

On the other hand, we are constantly bombarded with different news stories, often on the same news sites or in the same magazines, equally trading in fear, but this time fear about the decline of literacy in the sciences and mathematics. Again, what is interesting here is the way in which this fear is presented. Rarely if ever do these stories lament the decline of the sciences as a form of human practice and knowledge, rather the fear is always located in the *economic effects* of this decline. We are told that if our respective societies do not invest in better science and mathematics education then our economies will stagnate, since science and mathematics are the twin motors of innovation and innovation is what drives capitalism forward. So the imperative manifested by these fear-mongering stories about the decline of science is always about something external to the joys of doing science. It is concerned instead with the continued subjugation of the sciences to the demands of a capitalist economy, both in terms of producing new products but also in terms of producing new mathematical formulas for the abstract production of wealth through stock market trading, like those that were part of the 2008 collapse of the global economy. It is concerned, in a word, with techno-science rather than science as such.

Our everyday anxiety about the sciences has this double structure of fearing the worst that science can unleash on humanity and the rest of the planet while also being concerned that the sciences are chronically under-funded. This double anxiety displays the same logic as Woody Allen's joke in *Annie Hall* about the two old men eating at a Catskill resort. One says to the other, "Boy, the food at this place is really terrible." The other responds, "Yeah, and such small portions!"

But this double anxiety is just one half of a larger double relation that constitutes our confused idea of the sciences today. We can see in the anxiety over the decline of science and mathematics literacy that our society is also enamored with the sciences. This is expressed in the contemporary popularity of so-called "geek culture," with incredibly popular TV shows like *The Big Bang Theory* and less popular reality shows like *Beauty and the Geek* and *King of the Nerds*, websites like io9 and I Fucking Love Science, and popular science spokespersons like Neil deGrasse Tyson being fan favorites for talk shows and whose opinions on all matters, including political and social issues, are given special attention regardless of their level of knowledge in those fields. What is actually expressed in this infatuation of popular culture with geek culture? Clearly, we are still presented here with an image of science seen in the anxiety present in the other half of this double relation. That is, these shows offer us peeks into the lives of "those who are supposed to know," as Lacan referred to them. For when someone watches *The Big Bang Theory* or reads a journalistic account of some scientific discovery on io9 they are not concerned with the actual practice of science. They are either taken with the journalistic account itself, which almost always relies on the writing being accessible and playing on the reader's sense of wonder while actively disavowing this kind of sentimentalism in the practice of the discovery itself. Or, as with *The Big Bang Theory*, they are taken with the joy of looking behind the veil of the "subject supposed to know," looking into the remarkably similar and mundane lives of people who are thought to understand the secrets of the universe. How else are we to explain the popularity of an utter sociopath like *The Big Bang Theory*'s Sheldon except as a modern example of the figure of the bumbling priest, popular when religion held a stronger ideological place in society? *The Big Bang Theory* is to the science community what *Father Ted* was to the priesthood (though, perhaps, less funny).

Philosophy is not immune to this relation to science, structured in this double way. For it too has always had a certain obsession with the sciences and mathematics. This obsession stretches all the way back to the establishment of Plato's Academy, which famously is said to have had "Let no one ignorant of geometry enter" engraved above its doors, and can be seen today in the work of Alain Badiou, perhaps our greatest contemporary Platonist, with his equation of "mathematics = ontology" (to say nothing of the continued reign of "scientific naturalism" in mainstream Anglophone philosophy).[1] Nor is philosophy immune to the anxiety about science, as can be seen in the popularity of Heidegger's skepticism expressed in his famous statement, "Science does not think" (however nuanced the statement may be within the wider context).[2] So where can we situate Laruelle's relation to science with regard to this everyday and philosophical double relation? Answering that question will be the focus of this chapter. We will see that Laruelle offers us a much simpler relation to science as a kind of means, but the shape of this means as a posture or stance will give form to the practice of non-philosophy.[3] Science is then not treated as subordinate to non-philosophy, rather non-philosophy *is* science and philosophy identically, or in a unified theory.

This is a bold claim, but insisting on this intimate connection between philosophy and science is not particular to Laruelle. As he is aware and discusses explicitly in the first two chapters of *Principles of Non-Philosophy*, philosophy has always thought of itself in relation to science (either positively or negatively) and going back to Plato many philosophers have thought of philosophy itself as a science. However, the meaning behind this deceptively common term "science" needs to be uncovered, not only because its meaning in the history of philosophy and in the contemporary sciences is wildly different, but also because they both diverge somewhat from what Laruelle intends by the term.

The term science (the same in both English and French) is derived from the Latin *scientia*, which in antiquity referred to both philosophy and what we call the natural sciences today. In general the term was used to refer to any pursuit of knowledge that could be communicated to others and developed outside of a private experience or language. Someone can attain knowledge in the sciences by undertaking a science, but no one can actually see through the eyes of someone else or experience their desires or dreams or beliefs directly the way that person does. The Latin *scientia* literally means "knowledge," and the development of the concept was dependent upon the older Greek notion of knowledge, *epistemē*, from which we derive the term "epistemology." In both cases the roots of the idea are developed explicitly in terms we would not today recognize as scientific, but rather as philosophical. In the seventeenth century what was then termed "natural philosophy" began to develop in distinction from what was called "moral philosophy." Eventually natural philosophy became an autonomous branch of human knowledge and came to be called the natural sciences. The way we think of science now is largely determined by this division, established hundreds of years ago as science came to refer to any human knowledge concerned with the natural world. A kind of philosophical trick occurred around this time, rooted not in a scientific view but in the implicit philosophical view within science itself. That is, the idea of nature dominated the idea of science. Even today what is "natural" tends to be treated as the ultimate reference point for what is true. After all, nature is thought to be the realm of objectivity, or of what is real and remains real even when we do not perceive it ourselves, subjectively, as real. Science is thought to simply provide us with that objective knowledge. Simply put, knowledge and truth are situated together within science, assuming an unproblematic relationship between the two grounded in the objective realm of nature. A scientific statement, it is thought, can always be tested for its veracity.

Much of this understanding of the natural sciences is accurate, but much of it also remains very philosophical, even ideological in the sense that there is something unscientific hidden beneath our everyday image of science. To see this one only needs to look at our concept of nature itself and see that it is not necessarily a scientific concept. The conception of nature as objective in distinction to subjective is rooted in the philosophical distinction between subject and object. And nature as a concept is rarely explored by the natural sciences explicitly, as the meaning of the term is far murkier than an exact scientific inquiry would allow for. For nature could refer to the biological, the cosmological, the physical, the mathematical, and so on, but is not clearly a single object for any technical scientific discipline. In short, it is not clear what the term "nature" would refer to or how science would undertake an investigation of an object as massive and disparate as what is implied by the term "nature." Yet the idea of the natural undergirds so much of our everyday intellectual work. Nature and the natural are appealed to when deciding which economic theories are scientific, when deciding what political and ethical actions are realistic and rooted outside the apparent ideological coordinates of politics, and when deciding whose knowledge gets to count. In a very paradoxical sense, the Christian theological tradition of natural law persists largely unchanged within the secular milieu of the spontaneous philosophy of science found in the media.

Many contemporary theorists of science have gathered a body of evidence to show the ways in which science is often implicated within wider political and social systems that are themselves ignored by scientists in their practice. The example of nature given above is just one of many that these theorists have uncovered, and while the popular discourses on the sciences have not yet caught up to these theorists, Laruelle is formed by their tradition of critique. Critique in the best sense, not the erasing of science, but neither the betrayal of science that comes from treating it as if it were an unproblematic, finished project. Critique, rather, in the sense of attempting to understand science by uncovering its internal structure, seeing how it actually operates, what objects it can provide knowledge of, what aspects of it are overdetermined by political or economic or social systems, and perhaps help to free science from those systems so that it can realize its human promise in its practice. For ultimately science as knowledge is a promise. It says that, as human beings, we may know, we may engage with the wider world in a way that makes the world something other than a system of oppression.

For Laruelle this cannot happen through a merely philosophical critique like those of his forbears. The task now is to create a democracy-(of)-thought, one where philosophy doesn't come along and declare itself the savior of a science enslaved by capitalist techno-science, or present itself as some kind of ally to the promise of science and proceed to talk over it, overcoding scientific codes with philosophical ones. Some readers may wonder at the strange grapheme found in the phrase "democracy-(of)-thought." This is explained in the translators' introduction to *Principles of Non-Philosophy* and readers may look there for a longer technical discussion.[4] Ultimately, though, the formulation refers to a way of thinking that would be immanently democratic, where the democracy practiced is a way of thinking and the thinking itself is a democracy. This is the reason for placing the "of" between parentheses, a reference to the Husserlian practice of *bracketing* within phenomenology where you take some concept and *suspend* it, allowing the phenomenologist to investigate it with his or her presuppositions under erasure.

This true democracy-(of)-thought becomes the site where philosophy and science are equal parties within non-philosophy's unified theory of philosophy and science. Laruelle describes clearly this relationship of philosophy and the sciences within non-philosophy as one of equality when he writes:

Philosophy – to simplify here – is a simple a priori for science, but this is now a priority without primacy or domination. In what is no longer a new alliance of philosophy and science, philosophy is no longer judge and party, but simply a party like science. [...] It no longer has the claim of dominating or transcending science, but it is assured that, for this thought at least, non-philosophy, that *if* there is science, *then* its identity with it is determined-in-the-last-instance. It captures a universality or a generality that it did not spontaneously have.[5]

While various philosophies of science and epistemologies will provide Laruelle with the image of science, they do so without a fundamental investigation of philosophy's essence and so fall into a kind of dominating role with regard to science, as philosophy assumes itself the one true mouthpiece for the truths found therein. When they do attempt to investigate that essence they are unable to do so without simply doing philosophy again, always perpetuating what Laruelle calls the originary faith of philosophy or the Principle of Sufficient Philosophy (to be explored in the following section). If non-philosophy is to trace an escape route out of philosophy's authoritarianism, where it claims authority over the sciences and every other discipline, either as a grounding discourse or as what really underlies those disciplines, then it will be through this new unified theory of philosophy and science as a new democracy-(of)-thought. Laruelle does this by bringing together two different paradigms, one that he calls non-Husserlian and another he calls non-Gödelian. In the rest of this chapter I will focus on exploring the phenomenology of Husserl and the metascientific work of Gödel to show what Laruelle takes from them.

THE NON-HUSSERLIAN PARADIGM

Much of what is discussed by Laruelle in "'First Science' as Unified Theory of Science and Philosophy" is a deepening of the argument that we have already traced in our history of non-philosophy as the history of the conjugation of philosophy and science. Laruelle outlines the usual philosophical approaches to thinking about science which can be broken down into two main philosophical types to be distinguished from the unified theory of philosophy and science he will develop. The first of the standard philosophical types is said to be structured according to "epistemological Difference." Here the relationship is determined by the difference between philosophy and science. The second, which could take the name of "epistemological Identity," does away with this epistemological Difference between philosophy and science and instead identifies philosophy with science in some way. The most obvious contemporary example would be the philosophy of Alain Badiou, who claims that mathematics = ontology thereby turning philosophy into a practice of "meta-ontology."[6]

Neither of these two dominant philosophy-science structures is what Laruelle develops, though in his approach there will appear to be elements of both. From epistemological Difference he will take seriously the idea that philosophy and science have two distinct identities. From epistemological Identity he takes seriously the idea that philosophy provides a kind of "meta" statement. But instead of these philosophical statements constituting meta-ontological statements, they provide statements that are meta-scientific, which may be objects inside a science of philosophy itself, and which may also disclose the essence-(of)-science as well.[7] In both of the standard relationships between philosophy and science the structure is based upon the way identity and difference is distributed. The non-standard approach Laruelle will develop is also based upon the distribution of identity and difference, but in such a way as to avoid any confusing of the two. For this is now a democracy of thought, in which there are no longer two identities, but rather a single identity of the duality of science and philosophy. That is, the relationship between science and philosophy is not treated as either a mixing of identities between science and philosophy, nor is it based upon a difference between an epistemo-logy where there is an episteme (a regime of knowledge) and a logos (a logic or structure of that knowledge) distinct from one another. Now there is an equality between philosophy and science, no difference, but that suspension of difference comes through the identity of their duality.[8]

Laruelle goes on to explain that, "More generally non-philosophical democracy can no longer be a *principle* or a *telos*, a *first equality*, which is to say auto-positional, and finally an equality of essence which returns to philosophical difference. Equality is only realized as such, conserved too, if it is an effect rather than a principle; an effect of a radical identity rather than an auto-positional principle."[9] Which is to say that this equality is real precisely because it is an effect. What is it an effect of? Of the radical identity of the Real from which the duality between science and religion comes. Much of this will remain obscure until we have a handle on Laruelle's understanding of identity, which we will tackle in Chapter 4. But we can understand it as saying that the duality of science and philosophy is based upon the identity of the human who practices the two disciplines. This is what allows us to no longer have to think of science and philosophy as based upon a primary difference, and which also allows us to see that that they each have their own essence or identity relative to the radical identity of their equality before the Real.

The consequence of this equality is that neither science nor philosophy is adequate in itself to think that Real. For Laruelle this effectively shatters what he sees as the underlying urdoxa of philosophical perception, the philosophical faith in philosophy's ability to think everything. This notion of urdoxa, which can also be referred to as belief or even as faith, comes from Husserl who says that he introduces the term "as suitably expressing the intentional back-reference of all 'modalities of belief' which we previously have affirmed."[10] In other words, urdoxa functions a great deal like an axiom, but with one fundamental difference – its status as an axiom is veiled and so comes to function in an authoritarian way as a simple fideistic faith, though without even realizing it could be even labeled as such. By recognizing and pointing out this urdoxa, this originary faith of philosophy, Laruelle is able to negate philosophy's authoritarianism (in the sense that philosophy takes itself as the authority on whatever is philosophizable) and this negation leads to a new understanding of philosophy. In part this is what Laruelle takes from Husserl's paradigm of "philosophy as a rigorous science."

This attempt to locate what Laruelle calls the "identity of philosophy" is indebted to the Husserlian search for essences as a proclaimed scientific search. Thus when Laruelle comes to call the invariant structure of philosophy the Philosophical Decision he arrives there by way of what Husserl called eidetic variation. Dan Zahavi explains this succinctly: "According to Husserl, I can obtain an essential insight, a *Wesensschau*, if through an eidetic variation, I succeed in establishing the horizon within which the object can change without losing its identity as a thing of that type. In that case, I will have succeeded in disclosing the invariant structures that make up its essence."[11] Of course such variation is potentially endless and open to further description and further variation which may indeed end up changing our claims about the invariant structures that make up the essence of X. And this is precisely what we see in the development of Laruelle's work as regards the Identity of philosophy itself.

Now we have come to the point at which Laruelle thinks he makes a distinctive advance on Husserl. For this claim to be able to provide an Identity of philosophy as well as of science is very similar to the goal of the phenomenological reduction, to see the thing-in-itself. Husserl's concept was subject to constant evolution as he developed and refined the reduction, so that what first began as simply bracketing out the errors of psychologism began to become more and more complicated as the obfuscatory power of the natural attitude was progressively weakened and layer upon layer of imposed meaning was removed from the thing-in-itself. However, there is a sense that the question of ontology, the question of Being, remained operative in Husserl's work up to the final work that he published during his lifetime (for instance in his final text, *The Crisis of the European Sciences and Transcendental Philosophy*, he discusses the ontology of the life-world). For Laruelle this focus on Being is a symptom of the invariant structure of philosophy, its decisional character, attempting to bring something actual under the determination of some philosophically projected transcendence. Consider, with this in mind, Husserl's statement that:

> The relations between phenomenology and all other sciences [...] have their ground in this essential relation between *transcendental* and *transcendent* Being.

Their very meaning implies that the domain over which phenomenology rules extends in a certain remarkable way over all the other sciences from which it has none the less disconnected itself.[12]

What we see here, then, is a kind of philosophical faith that remains in Husserl's attempt to make philosophy a rigorous science, a faith that philosophy as phenomenology may rule, may set the criteria and speak for, the sciences below it by way of a transcendental and transcendent Being. Laruelle's own project is an advance over Husserl's in the disempowering of this faith even further, by subjecting philosophy, phenomenology included, to a reduction equal to the one performed on psychologism.

This then takes the form of a generalization of the phenomenological reduction to something akin to a "Real reduction." Rather than the return proclaimed by Husserl – a return to the "things themselves" in a sense assumed to refer to things or objects outside of philosophy – we are instead called to return to philosophy and science as things, to thought as a thing, and to think through their character without any hallucination or what is termed by Husserl the natural attitude. What is the natural attitude for a philosopher? The concept of the natural attitude is not immediately legible to those who assume "natural" refers to some biological determinism regarding how we perceive or take our surroundings. Instead, for Husserl, the natural attitude names the complex of what might be called in a Marxist register "ideologies" or in a Foucauldian register "epistemes." That is, the natural attitude is not "natural" in the sense of "just what is," but is a construction that comes to be forgotten as a construction. The ideology or episteme is the very structure by which we as observers of the world are able to make sense of it, and it is so fundamental to our "vision" that we no longer see it, much like people who wear contact lenses or glasses do not see these instruments of vision unless they do so intentionally or the glasses become so dirty that they can no longer see without distraction. In other words, the natural attitude is not natural in a straightforward sense, but only presents itself as "just what is." What then of our question, what is the natural attitude for a philosopher? One who, we might say, thinks they have bracketed this very natural attitude? Well, for Laruelle, it is simply that philosophy is sufficient to think the Real, that philosophy is sufficient to itself and may think itself, and that even if it requires some supplement, it will direct or drive that supplement's thinking. In short, philosophy's natural attitude is that philosophy may be a totality, that it may be complete. It is here that Laruelle thinks Husserl's project find its real supplement – the one that can break the philosophical faith found even in radical phenomenology

– in the work of Gödel, who both showed the incompleteness of systems and created an ingenious form of translation which Laruelle will take up in a non-philosophical register.

THE NON-GÖDELIAN PARADIGM

For many readers of *Principles of Non-Philosophy* the invocation of the famous mathematician and logician Kurt Gödel may appear puzzling, especially if they are familiar with Laruelle's more recent critique of Badiou, published as *Anti-Badiou*, where the latter's philosophy is criticized for its reliance on a Principle of Sufficient Mathematics. Of course this Principle of Sufficient Mathematics is formally the same as the Principle of Sufficient Philosophy, where one discourse is taken to be adequate or able to encompass knowledge of the Real. Some may suspect that Laruelle is here doing the same thing he accuses Badiou of doing, that is, invading a science and setting in motion an authoritarian plan that makes that science subservient to philosophical demands. But whereas *Anti-Badiou* is a bold polemic, aping in many ways Badiou's own polemical style, *Principles of Non-Philosophy* is an intricately constructed work. The use of Gödel is neither an invocation of a scientific work to bolster unscientific philosophical claims nor an authoritarian invasion of a science by philosophy in order to direct that science to purely philosophical ends. Rather, a non-Gödelian paradigm is invoked by Laruelle to complete the non-Husserlian paradigm and thereby show the complete shape of non-philosophy as a unified theory of philosophy and science.

For Laruelle, Gödel provides the answer for the corollary, antinomic question to the one presented by Husserl (how does science come to philosophy?): how does thought come to science? But, more importantly, with regard to disempowering the authoritarian impulse in philosophy he asks how can philosophy or the generalization of philosophy as non-philosophy speak of science while avoiding the standard philosophy of science and epistemology and their attendant problems?[13] To understand what this means we will need first to look at how these standard forms of philosophy of science and epistemology are structured according to Laruelle, and how this structure is undercut by Gödel's famous incompleteness theorems.

Laruelle is clear throughout this chapter that non-philosophy must be philosophy and science at the same time and to do so it must take science as an object alongside of philosophy. For Laruelle this conception of science has to be of what he calls the *identity-(of)-science* or alternatively the *essence-(of)-science*.[14] This identity-(of)-science is of course science in itself, rather than the construction of science found in various philosophies of science which always split the image of science into an idea of Science-with-a-capital-S and the specific sciences like biology, mathematics, physics, and so on. But this attempt to construct a theory of the essence-(of)-science poses a challenge for Laruelle. On the one hand, he rejects the treatment of the sciences one may find in Latour and others where the sciences are presented as practices whose games of will to knowledge and power are obscured and which "science studies" may uncover. This kind of philosophy of science, with its social sciences supplement, has already been touched upon in our earlier discussion of the relationship between science and techno-science. Without taking an unnecessary detour through a Latourian understanding of science, we can see that Laruelle's eidetic variation of science to allow the essence-(of)-science to appear operates in a very different register. Laruelle's project is "transcendental" in the sense found in phenomenology and mutated by non-philosophy, meaning that it aims to find an identity of science in itself rather than delineate the various forms of science through their empirical characteristics. So Laruelle does not treat the products of science ready for general consumption in the marketplace, he is not concerned with thinking from the image of science present in the capture of science in capitalist techno-science. And, yet on the other hand, he is explicit that he is not looking for the Idea or *eidos* of Science-with-a-capital-S in a purely Platonic sense as separate from the actuality of the sciences. His goal is to think, then, the essence-(of)-science as the practice of science, not eternal and unchanging, but as it is lived, without splitting it within thought.

Epistemology, or the theory of the grounding of secure scientific knowledge, is fundamentally structured along such a split between the practical realities of the sciences and the Idea of Science-with-a-capital-S. Laruelle signals this fundamentally split structure in the way he writes about epistemology as "epistemo-logy." This expresses what Laruelle sees as the founding gesture of epistemology, which posits a "distance" or "difference" between *episteme* and *logos* or the knowledge produced by science and the Idea that regulates the identity of that production as scientific.[15] This difference is what structures the attempt to ground the sciences in a philosophically or theoretically rigorous way, or what Laruelle will now call *metascience*, as well as what produces the philosophy of science that attempts to tell us what the essence of science is, or what Laruelle will now call *metascientific*.[16] Metascience will be retained as already found within the sciences, meaning that they do not need epistemology or philosophy of science to provide this ground, while metascientific discourses will be turned into a material for non-philosophy to use rather than an actual discourse revealing the essence of science.

To understand the concept of metascience we can now turn more explicitly to Gödel, because the term metascience is derived by Laruelle from another mathematician, David Hilbert, and his conception of metamathematics. Metamathematics is an important component in understanding what Gödel did with his incompleteness theorems, and to understand it one only need to consider a mathematical formula. The formula can be as simple as an equation learned during childhood like $2 + 2 = 4$, or it may be of a level of complexity accessible only to those who have studied advanced mathematics, for example a relatively simple but likely opaque equation such as '$(\exists x)\,(x = sy)$' (we will explain this equation a little later in the chapter). $2 + 2 = 4$ may seem like it has meaning, but that is simply a trick played upon the reader by the familiarity one has with this arithmetic equation. The second equation is relatively simple for those who have studied logic and mathematics, but for many readers who have not had much instruction in these fields it will present itself as a meaningless string of symbols. And, mathematically, it is a meaningless string of symbols! But what is important to keep in mind is that $2 + 2 = 4$ is also a meaningless string of symbols. What does it mean to say that strings of mathematical formula are meaningless, including one that seems so obviously meaningful? When you look at $2 + 2 = 4$ you are performing metamathematics simultaneously in your head, because you are bestowing this meaningless string with a meaning which can be translated into normal language as, say, two of X added to two more of X equals four of X. This is what Hilbert's metamathematics refers to – language about mathematics. The statements produced by this language of metamathematics are not found within mathematics itself.

To see this more clearly let us consider our more complicated example, which comes from Bertrand Russell and Alfred North Whitehead's *Principia Mathematica*, to which Gödel was responding to in his paper "On Formally Undecidable Propositions of *Principia Mathematica* and Related Systems," where his incomplete theorems were published.[17] Taking the formula '$(\exists x)\,(x = sy)$' we can again translate it into language that is meaningful. Literally it would be translated as "there is an *x* such that *x* is the immediate successor of *y*" and we could go on to explain that, for example, this formula accounts logically for the normal number 2 following the normal number 1. But that meaning isn't there in the formula itself, which is not written in English and so necessarily cannot produce a meaningful English statement (or whatever language is being used outside of mathematics to speak about mathematics). The formula requires translation for it to be meaningful and such translation is always readily available. Within itself mathematics is active and works without the need for this ordinary operation of meaning in a language outside of itself.

To understand what metamathematics has to do with the incompleteness of systems one must consider that mathematics is considered to be a deductive system. This means that theoretically mathematics requires nothing other than itself to develop. Therefore, if mathematics could be shown to be simply a subset of logic then developing the logical axioms that ground mathematics would suffice for the development of a totality of true statements. This was indeed the goal of many nineteenth- and twentieth-century philosophers and logicians before Gödel, foremost amongst them Russell and Whitehead as represented in their 1910 *Principia Mathematica*. However, what Gödel shows is that this is ultimately false, since there is no certainty that these complex systems do not contain internal contradictions, as the principles themselves have to become so complex as to belie any certainty.[18] This carries with it a corollary conclusion that is itself revolutionary in stating that all formal systems within which arithmetic can be developed, like that of *Principia Mathematica*, are essentially incomplete and that such incompleteness is related to that system's consistency.[19] I will provide a very truncated explanation of how Gödel's theorem worked before turning back to its use for Laruelle.

Let us begin by first taking the title of Gödel's paper where he published his famous proofs, "On Formally Undecidable Propositions of *Principia Mathematica* and Related Systems," and work our way backwards. First, as already noted, the proof takes up *Principia Mathematica* as the primary system it engages with. That is, it will show the incompleteness of the system represented by *Principia Mathematica* in particular, but Gödel is emphatic at the end of his paper that this theorem works for any attempt to prove the consistency of a formal system for this consistency will fail to be formally demonstrated since it is always undecidable from within the formal system or calculus deployed.[20] This is the meaning of the first part of the title, where undecidability refers to the result that, from within the formal system, neither a positive proposition (say "this calculus is consistent") nor its negation ("this calculus is not consistent") is demonstrable within that formal calculus. If they were demonstrable then that system would be inconsistent. What Gödel shows is that if a system like *Principia Mathematica* (PM) is to be consistent then it will necessarily be incomplete.

To prove this rather remarkable statement, Gödel used an ingenious form of mapping, one in which Russell and Whitehead's formal logical notation and their metamathematical statements were mapped onto a new arithmetic notation system. The process itself is inspired as it takes one meaningless string of mathematical notation and translates it into another equally meaningless string, but this new system is arithmetic, meaning that a complex string like '$(\exists x)(x = sy)$' can be translated into a simple arithmetic equation where each of the signs can be translated into what are referred to as Gödel numbers (see Figure p. 40).[21]

(	∃	x	)	(	x	=	s	y	)
↓	↓	↓	↓	↓	↓	↓	↓	↓	↓
8	4	13	9	8	13	5	7	17	9

In essence, these Gödel numbers allow for the original formula to be represented by a *single* number corresponding to that original formula, representing within an arithmetic calculus itself *both* the metamathematical statement and the logical notation behind that statement. Such a number may be very large and so may also be referred to by a simpler symbol like *m*.

Now we can begin to follow the main outlines of Gödel's argument. First, he showed that PM can be used to construct a formula that represents the metamathematical statement, "The formula is not demonstrable using the rules of PM." This is somewhat like the Liar's Paradox, which presents the statement "I, the liar, am lying." This paradox arises because the liar is telling the truth about his being a liar, contradicting the claim that he is a liar. In other words we are given something that is both true and not true at the same time. In the same way the formula constructed by Gödel says *of itself* that it is not demonstrable. Let us call this formula ("This formula is not demonstrable") formula G and the single Gödel number that can be associated with it *g*. It would now be a metamathematical statement within Gödel's system saying, "The formula that has the Gödel number *g* is not demonstrable."

This brings us to the second move, where Gödel shows that this formula G is demonstrable if and only if its formal negation (not G) is also demonstrable. This is written into the formula itself, since in order to demonstrate the truth of a statement that says, "The formula is not demonstrable," one has to demonstrate that statement itself. But this means that for the general system itself to be consistent then this statement must be formally undecidable, since to be consistent both its positive statement and its negation cannot be demonstrated. Furthermore, if PM is consistent neither G nor its negation can be derived from the axioms of PM, since both contain their own negation.

Thus far, nothing more has really been added except a mapping into a new formal system of the same problem expressed in the Liar's Paradox. But this, the third step, is where Gödel's insight begins to move past the simply undecidable to show the incompleteness of the logical system attempting to ground the science of mathematics. For Gödel shows that, while formula G is not formally demonstrable, it is nevertheless a true *arithmetical* formula, as he demonstrates using arithmetic mapping of the logical notation and metamathematical statements. This leads to the fourth step, wherein formula G is shown to be both true and formally undecidable and thus leads to the conclusion that PM is incomplete. Or, in other words, since this proposition and its negation are undecidable, PM is unable to deduce all arithmetical truths from the axioms and rules of PM as expressed logically. Gödel goes on to demonstrate that even if PM were complicated by ever more axioms then a new formula G' could be constructed *ad infinitum*.

And this brings us to the fifth step of his conclusion. Gödel then constructed a formula A that represents the metamathematical statement "PM is consistent." This is then written in formal notation in relation to formula G (A $\supset$ G or "formula A if and only if formula G"). He then went on to show that this set is formally demonstrable within PM. Therefore the consistency of PM cannot be mirrored within the formal reasoning that PM itself constitutes as a system.[22] To put it in other words, "If PM is consistent, then it is incomplete," or "PM is consistent if and only if there is at least one formula of PM that is not demonstrable inside PM."[23]

I would invite the reader to consult both Gödel's original paper and the accessible introduction to it provided by Nagel and Newman for a longer exposition that will undoubtedly help elucidate what is happening in Gödel at more length and with more attention than our purposes allow for here.[24] What is important in this work is that the reader understands the very broad strokes of Gödel's proofs, seeing how he accomplishes this disempowering of what Laruelle calls the metascientific through a metascience. The operation Gödel uses to do this is the modeling of these metascientific statements into arithmetic Gödel numbers, which translates the metascientific statements into an object for science (rather than an object for philosophy) elucidating the identity- or essence-(of)-science.[25] It is important to note that Laruelle does not attempt to appropriate the findings of the incompleteness theorems for any philosophical purpose. He does not attempt to show that science *needs* philosophy or even that philosophy *needs* science in order to be complete. Rather, he credits Gödel with discovering a form of quasi-reflexivity that is not philosophical, showing that science is *index sui* or is able to think without the need for a paternalistic philosophy of science. Laruelle sees an opening here for a non-Gödelianism grounded on what he calls a transcendental identity, such that Gödel may now be used in a philosophical way, but without philosophical appropriation or overcoding. That is, in the way that Gödel was able to take and transform metascientific statements, which present as philosophical statements as well, into scientific (arithmetic) statements through a kind of translation that was able to actually represent the metascientific statement and think differently at the same time.

41

FROM SPONTANEOUS PHILOSOPHY AND PHILOSOPHY AS A RIGOROUS SCIENCE TO A UNIFIED THEORY OF PHILOSOPHY AND SCIENCE

These two paradigms thought together allow Laruelle to think science and philosophy democratically. The reflexive translation of science and metascience in Gödel is generalized so that philosophy may be translated into scientific terms and vice versa. This is why we find Laruelle writing that non-philosophy has a scientific character in a way very different from epistemology:

> We deal with the characteristics generally assumed to belong to science "in itself", through a transcendental exigency, without the mixture of epistemological Difference, without being able to know if it truly concerns the essence of science. It is the same for philosophy's assumed essence, of which we can only know the already philosophical. This is why we have used the scientific hypothesis, the axiomatic method, induction and deduction, but also the transcendental and philosophical a prioris, in order to construct the proper instruments of non-philosophy, i.e. of a discipline that does not yet exist, which thus had to be discovered and some of whose tools we have tried to gather.[26]

This aspect of Laruelle's non-philosophy nuances what might seem like a straightforward essentialism in his searching for identities and essences. Here we see that an identity or an essence is not a unitary object, vacuum sealed and static, but instead has a kind of "insufficient consistency" or is unified much in the same way that a human life has an identity or consistency to it without that consistency being static or anything other than "lived." How else does a democracy function except as the mutual translation of one desire into another, through the interplay and mutation of particularities, that is *identities*, that are nonetheless unified even if in nothing but their discourse together.

This *lived* aspect of a unified theory is vital for understanding the way that Laruelle's mutation of epistemology is part and parcel of a kind of discourse of liberation. While the "non-" of non-philosophy signifies a mutation and not a negation, there is a certain sense in which the "non" is also a simple French "no." But a "no" to philosophy as refusal of philosophy's sufficiency or proclaimed authority, just as it is a no to Science-witha-capital-S's proclaimed authority as seen in the spontaneous philosophy of science found in the media. But this relative "no" is a yes to the liberation of philosophy and science from their hallucinated authoritarian forms. A "no" in favor of the liberation of the lived experience (*vécu*) of thinking philosophically or scientifically, which these forms of thought can come to dominate and turn into golems that destroy the very human beings who brought those forms of thinking into being. *Vécu* is a notoriously difficult word to translate into English, though most people simply go with "lived experience," and this often makes sense since it is related to the German *Erlebnis*. *Vécu*, a very common term in Laruelle's work repeated throughout *Principles of Non-Philosophy*, but seen in his earliest works to his most recent, is the past participle of *vivre* or "to live," but this has the sense also of "living through." Now past participles are very important in Laruelle's various formulations. So, let's take a phenomenological example: he often speaks of the given-without-givenness, the seen-without-sight, and so in *Principles of Non-Philosophy* we tended to translate *vécu* with the somewhat strange sounding "lived" to make sense of his formulation *vécu-sans-vie* or "lived-without-life." In each case, the point is to free the actualized, immanent identity from its transcendental conception, always, for Laruelle, actually dependent upon and projected from the actualized identity. And this, for Laruelle, is precisely what philosophy does – it claims to think some actual thing and ends up projecting and circumscribing these actuals in closed concepts within a transcendence, confusing one actual, the transcendent term, with another in a reversibility of actual and transcendent that Laruelle describes as "antidemocracy."[27]

What then defines this inter-translation of philosophy and science within a non-philosophical unified theory? The taking up of codes that become common to the two or at least able to be enacted in a philosophical or a scientific register. Laruelle puts it this way:

> If philosophy enters into a unified theory in so far as it is intrinsically a science, it must be able to operate through induction and deduction – rather than through interpretation – but transcendental induction and deduction, or relating to a priori knowledges on the very mode where induction and deduction relate to the objects of knowledge. If science enters into a unified theory in so far as it is intrinsically a philosophy, it must be able to operate through and upon the a priori knowledges, by way of a *universal* "condition" or "conditioning" rather than by general and regional laws; equally through transcendental operations which are ultimately operations of the *usage* of these universal knowledges.[28]

What we see here is that concepts normally thought to apply to science alone or to philosophy alone are said to be carried within the identity of each other as brought together in a unified theory and so these concepts may be redeployed in uses that are similar but ultimately heterogeneous. Within a unified theory difference is not erased, so a unified theory is not a synthesis, but a new identity is formed or "cloned" according to the difference and sameness between the two.

A unified theory is distinguished starkly from a standard philosophy of X, where X may be religion, ethics, aesthetics, or, as is paramount in

Principles of Non-Philosophy, science. Laruelle marks this starkness when he writes that "A unified theory is always expressed in the identity of a so-called transcendental equation, not a mathematical one, which nonetheless is a quasi-scientific object. A philosophy on the other hand is expressed in a tautology or a repetition."[29] To say that philosophy is a tautology or a repetition is to say that the X in the formula "philosophy of X" is no longer anything but a mirror for philosophy. The object it claims to speak of ends up simply being a reflection of the philosophy claiming to think it. Whereas to say that a unified theory is a transcendental equation is to make use of the non-Gödelian paradigm explored earlier. That is, a unified theory comes to mark an identity that itself is no longer simply a philosophy or a science but a new kind of object with a new kind of function, much in the same way that the equations in Gödel changed their function depending on the form they took, either formal or metamathematical.

3

The Subject is Not a Thinking Thing But the Force-(of)-Thought

In Rocco Gangle's useful thematic overview of Laruelle's oeuvre he traces the various developments of Laruelle's non-philosophy. There he tells us that, "Perhaps the main unanswered question for the works of Philosophy II (and among these, *Philosophies of Difference*) is the precise status of the philosophical *subject* as transformed within the theoretical stance of non-philosophy."[1] *Principles of Non-Philosophy*, along with the other three books collected under the periodization "Philosophy III," is a sustained and deliberate response to the question of the status of the philosophical subject as recast by non-philosophy. Why, though, would there be such a question? What is the importance of the philosophical subject and why would non-philosophy need to recast it? Answering these questions will be the focus of this chapter as we map out the influences and arguments in Chapter 3 of *Principles of Non-Philosophy* entitled "Unified or 'Non-Cartesian' Theory of the Subject: Duality of the Ego and the Subject." The title already tells the reader much about what will be argued and discussed in this chapter, for we see that Laruelle's use of unified theory will be important here, which always involves bringing together two identities without a synthesis of those identities, but as an identity of their difference and sameness. It is important to note that this identity is not taken as some third thing that would hold these two together in some "natural" dialectic, as well as to understand that a unified theory is not the creation of some new "thing" that supersedes the other two terms. It simply traces or models the ways in which they are confused by their sameness and their difference, the way that philosophy mixes them together to reflect philosophy's own "mixed" constitution of difference and identity, transcendence and immanence, and in this way a unified theory takes the scientific posture towards its object.

What we then see in the move from Chapter 2 to Chapter 3 of *Principles of Non-Philosophy* is a move from the way in which a unified theory may

45

be deployed as a general method (the unified theory of philosophy and science as the translation of scientific and philosophical methodologies) and as a specific modeling of some object (the unified theory of the Ego and the subject we are about to look at). In actuality, while one is clearly seen as method and the other as a kind of "object study," in both cases it is a matter of thinking the two as objects of a kind, for in non-philosophy philosophy becomes an object of study or a "non-object" to be theorized. Not as a norm-setting process akin to metaphilosophy, but in something more akin to the way science approaches objects – but a science shorn of its metaphysical presuppositions. A perhaps more direct example of what this looks like is the way in which biblical studies changed the way the Christian Bible was approached. Many credit Spinoza with inaugurating the critical study of (Judeo-Christian) scripture in his *Theologico-Political Treatise*, where scripture was no longer held as the arbiter of the true, but instead subject to some kind of truth beyond it. This turned "the Book" into another book, though we should avoid modifying this statement by saying "just another book" since one book among other books still has value in Spinoza and the tradition of biblical studies, much in the way that philosophy will still have value in non-philosophy even when it is shorn of its self-sufficient faith in the philosophizability of all things.

Laruelle begins to investigate the relationship of the Ego and the subject in philosophy, as part of his investigation of philosophy as an object through the lens of a unified theory of philosophy and science that relativizes philosophy but still recognizes its relative value. He says that since this involves "a theory of the object 'philosophy' and not a philosophical theory of empirical objects ... consequently a theory of the subject in our sense will be concerned less with the objects of the philosophy and sciences of the subject than with our manner of knowing a priori these new 'objects', these philosophies and sciences themselves."[2] The reader will therefore find at the start of Laruelle's chapter a short history of the way in which the subject and the Ego have been conceived in the history of philosophy and theory. Here Laruelle marks a difference between "theories of the subject" and "philosophies of the subject," though both find their origins in Cartesian philosophy. Laruelle is quick to note that there is a difference between Descartes and the tradition that followed him in quite complex ways in the philosophies of Kant, Fichte, Hegel, Nietzsche, Husserl, and others.[3] But in fact, it is this assumed "supersession" of Descartes in these critiques of his conception of the "cogito" that leads to the choice between a theory of the subject or a philosophy of the subject. Laruelle thus vacillates here, at times presenting a history of the subject and the Ego with their attendant critiques, and at other times providing his own unified theory of the subject and the Ego. Importantly it is this history that provides the material for his theory. The reader should then approach Laruelle's sketching of this history as part of the material development of his own non-philosophical theory – rather than reading it as a history of philosophy as such, approach it as something more akin to a typology, a term he himself uses in this chapter. A typology then that traces the kind of broad moves or structures at play here between the two approaches.

What marks the difference between the two approaches is how the subject is thought to be apprehended or understood. For theories of the subject present a "scientifically skewed treatment" using "mathematico-psychoanalytic" means that "culminate in objectifying [the subject], dividing it and dispersing it to the brink of the void."[4] Laruelle here is referring to the theoretical work of Lacan and Althusser, who used formalizing techniques in their theoretical investigation of philosophical concepts. This formalist approach is not scientific in the sense that a current Anglophone reader of philosophy may expect, such as can be found in the theories of subjectivity being developed in neurophilosophy, which looks to cognitive science for answers to philosophical problems. But what this French formalist approach shares in common with Anglophone neurophilosophy is its treatment of the subject as an object to be known or expressed through some kind of mathematical or psychoanalytic means.[5]

The other and opposed approach to the subject "orients itself toward an undivided immanence of the Ego" that is absolutely philosophical and without appeal to the sciences.[6] Here we find Husserl and Henry named, and indeed we could even include Heidegger, for what is expressed in these philosophies of the subject (as Ego) is a suspicion regarding the ability of science to provide knowledge of the undivided, immanent subject (as Ego), or even a charge that science covers up true knowledge through its objectification of the subject. The division between these two approaches is usually cast as a choice between a new form of rationalism and a new form of holistic philosophy, with various reasons given for or against. Sometimes those reasons are couched in terms that represent a kind of culture war within philosophy and theory, where one side is presented as pro-science and the other as opening to a new kind of irrational barbarism; or, one side is presented as in favor of a more peaceful, ethical way of being and the other as opening up to a new kind of technocratic barbarism. What is interesting to note is that Laruelle does not present them as a choice, but as an antinomy or as two mutually apparent or plausible approaches to the subject. What is needed is not a choice, for each position is rife with philosophical decisions, but treating each approach as a material that may be useful in rethinking the subject and the Ego in a pragmatic fashion beyond that antinomy.

With this in mind we may now be in a better position to understand the aim of the chapter, which Laruelle claims is a unified theory of the subject that "concerns substituting a new economy of the lived (Ego) and thought (subject) for the Ego/subject amphibology (Ego as subject and vice versa), but more profoundly still, a new economy of the Ego-without-subject and the subject-in-Ego, grounding it on their identity, but an identity-without-blend."[7] In other words, moving beyond the antinomy of a theory of the subject or a philosophy of the subject involves locating the actual identities or essences (in the non-essentialist sense Laruelle intends) of these two terms. Such a tracing of identities will involve recognizing the importance of something like an undivided life – though without the romanticism of Henry, so Laruelle will refer to "the lived-without-life," and without any appeal to the transcendent wholeness of lived experience – as well as recognizing the power of a certain kind of reason and formalism for constructing a theory of knowledge as a theory of subjectivity. We have already seen the importance of the concept of the lived for Laruelle, here represented by the Ego as cast in phenomenology. What is incumbent upon us now is to understand is the importance for non-philosophy of the second identity, the subject as thought or, more accurately, as force-(of)-thought.

In the remainder of this chapter we will trace the usual importance of the subject for standard philosophy. We will then turn to the way in which the subject and the Ego are confused in philosophy through the dyad of thought and Being, before looking at the way in which Laruelle seeks to separate them without recourse to an equally hallucinatory formalism. This then allows him to develop his conception of the subject, not as substance or quasi-object as the bearer of consciousness, but as force-(of)-thought. The latter is a concept of vital importance in non-philosophy and the following sections will help the reader gain a foothold in their attempts to understand it.

THE SUBJECT AND THE EGO IN STANDARD PHILOSOPHY

Why is the subject important in philosophy generally? If one had to find a thread with which to weave together the entire history of philosophy, one could use the ways in which the subject and the object have been conceived from Plato and Aristotle to Derrida and Adorno. Weaving such a story would be easy if it were cast and had its characters move and interact in the setting of epistemology, considered to have special importance for the philosophy of science and the relationship between the scientist (subject) and their various objects of study. For epistemology is concerned with knowledge, but knowledge understood to occur precisely in the relationship between an object that may be known by a subject through some kind of interaction that is either abstract (as in mathematics or theoretical physics broadly) or through sense perception (as in the empirical sciences broadly, like biology or ecology). Importantly, the subject is traditionally taken to be that which is able to know, either actively or passively, and the object is taken to be that which can be known.

These two terms, subject and object, are major aspects of the development of philosophy, but of course they also are familiar to us from the grammar of our everyday speech. This means that anyone unfamiliar with the classical or contemporary technical debates regarding the subject and object in philosophy may simply cast their mind back to common grammar lessons and consider the way their everyday speech is broken down. In a simple English sentence there will be a subject, an object, and a verb. For example, to take a familiar, if somewhat bewildering example from the history of philosophy, in the sentence "the cat is on the mat" the cat is the subject, the act of being someplace in space is the action, and the mat is the object. The subject is the bearer of an action *in relation* to an object which in some way "receives" or "bears" the action of the subject.

This *relation* of the object and the subject is an example of what Laruelle identifies as a mixed dualism that runs throughout philosophy, allowing for a reversibility of subject and object at the level of thought. We could even say that this relation is irreducible since the very conception of an object requires, in the history of philosophy, a subject to see it. While, as Olivier Boulnois summarizes for us, the term object and our understanding of it did not exist for the ancient Greeks in the form it does for us, the term that is translated as "object" in our contemporary translations of Aristotle, for example, was *antikeimenon* or simply "opposites." This relates back to the Latin term *obiici* and its various forms that mean, in sum, "something presenting itself as opposite or standing over against."[8] While this original meaning implied an obstacle, through a combination of Augustine's influential epistemology of active vision (where vision is directed outwards and not passively acting) and the ways in which this epistemology came to change the interpretation of Aristotle's theory of powers, it came to be that the object, now *obiecta*, was no longer just an obstacle, but also now "clearly recognized as the theme specific to the act of knowing."[9] In other words, the mainstream of philosophy came to see that what is known is no longer the thing as it actually is in itself, but the thing as it presents itself to a subject, or an actor which projects its vision onto the object and receives a reflection of that vision back. This clarification of the terms at play allowed philosophers to clarify the problem of knowledge as it presents itself as the question of how an object may be known by a subject, if at all, which is one of the major problems driving Kant's philosophy and post-Kantian philosophy generally.

For Kant the subject came to be the site upon which an understanding of this relationship had to center. For the subject is that thing that has to have access to the object in order to think it, yet the very nature of that access must lie in the constitution of the subject. That is, the subject, which lies opposite the object, does not stand in a relationship to the object as just another object. Such a relationship would require no consciousness or awareness of the object. Rather, the subject as subject may direct an action towards the object, of which awareness is one such action that may be deepened into an active knowledge or knowing. The locus of knowledge is not then located in the object, which may be known but is not the thing that knows, but in the subject, which is the bearer of the action and thus the constitution or condition of such knowledge. For philosophies of the subject and their attendant epistemologies, the subject comes to be the very basis for scientific knowledge; so to understand the constitution of the subject is to understand how knowledge and science are possible as well as to understand how science is practiced by subjects.

Yet it is here, in Kant's reading of Descartes, that we begin to see what Laruelle terms the amphibology of Ego and subject, and how the terms are simply reversible. The history of this reversibility goes back in part to the way in which Kant blended together Descartes' conception of the Ego (simply meaning "I," an ipseity, or the identity of oneself as distinct from others like "him" or "God") with his own conception of the subject. Kant's conception of the subject brings together the logical or grammatical sense discussed above with this notion of an ipseity or I. The subject, then, in Kant's sense, is both a kind of logical function and a self, which for him leads to a transcendental illusion where the subject is taken as an object which that same subject can know in itself, but since it is projected as an object it is only actually able to know it as represented and not in itself.[10] Ultimately, though, Laruelle points us to the fact that even this Kantian blending of Ego and subject takes root from a particular reading of Descartes, and so his tracing of the general structure of this blending together, even while highlighting and spelling out its post-Kantian developments, will circle around the Cartesian structure of the *cogito* as captured in the philosophical formula: "*ego cogito, ergo sum*," or, famously, "I think, therefore I am."

The triad of terms is the particular form within Cartesian philosophy of the generic and invariant Philosophical Decision, a concept that is not explored in depth here but which refers generally to the manner in which philosophy parses some phenomenon in a way that is reversible, according to Laruelle.[11] The general form of the Philosophical Decision is presented here as the economy of the "Dyad + One." In this case *ego, cogitatio, esse* refer to the dyad of thought (*cogitatio*) and being (*esse*), which are two contraries united in the hallucinated form of the One that philosophy's version of the Ego is. Concepts – or again "first names," as distinguished from philosophical concepts by the way they function in non-philosophy – that take the function of the uniting term in a philosophy between a fundamental dualism are cast by Laruelle as hallucinated forms of the One, which for him names the radical immanence beyond philosophical dualisms like thought and being or Being and Alterity, or even relative immanence and transcendence.

Laruelle's account of philosophy's internal functioning according to his description of Philosophical Decision has often been taken by unsympathetic readers as overly broad. While fully demonstrating this functioning would require a massive empirical undertaking, Laruelle aims for his project to be a transcendental description of philosophy's functioning akin to the way Kant and Husserl understood their projects to be about the description of the transcendental structures of knowing. Importantly, transcendental in this sense is not separate from the immanence of a thing but refers to its structures and conditions, and Laruelle attempts in his most recent works, notably *Philosophie non-standard*, to change the sense of this term in a subtle manner by employing the neologism "immanental." So what the Philosophical Decision aims to describe is precisely the invariant functioning of anything that would rightly be called philosophy, rather than providing a plethora of individual empirical readings that would illustrate it. However, in this case, where an empirical example from the history of philosophy is given, it is worthwhile to note that Laruelle's conception of Philosophical Decision can be seen to be supported by at least one other major philosopher's historical reading of Descartes, that of Jean-Luc Marion.

Marion is a well-known phenomenologist who is often grouped together with other French phenomenologists who have turned their attention to explicitly theological themes. Marion's own work, however, is more far-reaching in scope, with phenomenological inquiries into theological problematics, but also important research into the foundational concepts of phenomenology and historical studies that look to connect the contemporary phenomenological tradition to the traditions of modern and medieval philosophy. The influence of Marion's work for Laruelle has been largely overlooked, and it is true that Marion's conservative approach to classical phenomenology does not at first look to be in step with Laruelle. However, his theological work can clearly be seen at play in Laruelle's own engagement with religion, and Marion's conception of and investigation of the concept of givenness is vitally important for Laruelle's own conception of the "given-without-givenness." Furthermore, Marion's historical work on Descartes appears to operate as a background source for Laruelle's work in *Principles of Non-Philosophy*.[12] What Marion shows in that historical work is that the cogito is a mediating term, a term that precisely mediates thought and being. In mediating thought and being the Ego introduces itself as a third term: "It falls to the *ego* to mediate the equivalence between thought and Being metaphysically, in that, on the one hand, it thinks, and on the other, it is; but above all, it accomplishes this mediation because it introduces a third term: itself, no longer as undetermined *res cogitans*, but as substance residing in itself, spoken of in terms of itself."[13] More important than the way the ego is made into a kind of substance is the way the ego becomes the principle for the unity of thought and being. Again, this is an important constitutive move in philosophy for Laruelle, and here Marion draws upon Hegel's recognition that it is precisely where the Ego names the unity of thought and being that metaphysics begins:

> In the long exposition that the *Lectures on the History of Philosophy* will devote to Descartes some twenty years later, when Hegel wants to illustrate the definition that "metaphysics is what reaches after substance," he will retrieve the same interpretation of the conventional statement: "The determination of Being is in my 'I'; this connection is itself the first matter. Thought as Being and Being as thought – that is my certainty, 'I'; [this is] the celebrated *cogito ergo sum*." The utterance must be interpreted as recording the experience, concerned with a particular fact, of the universal principle of the "unity of Being and thought," a principle with which "we for the first time begin to consider his metaphysics." Cartesian thought becomes metaphysical when the "cogito sum" reveals the identity of Being and thought.[14]

Historically Marion's reading could be grouped along with those that read Descartes as substantializing the ego, a reading that popularly originates with Kant and that is contested by other scholars of Descartes' philosophy. However, such debates are not at play in Laruelle's reading and for the sake of advancing his argument he does not need to take a position regarding the historical question of Descartes' work. Ultimately, regardless of whether the Ego is at work as substance or as a kind of logical operator, what Marion's historical analysis shows is that one of these terms will be repeated, such that, in the Cartesian example here taken up by Hegel, when the Ego that thinks is "given" it also comes to be "thought," or as Laruelle writes, "Philosophy assumes that to give = to think, so much so that thought is given or occurs twice."[15] In this repetition of itself through the terms, this conception of the Ego does not come to reveal the identity of thought and being, but rather to confuse them as convertible within the thinking being that the Ego is.

Laruelle's conception of the Ego will attempt to break this economy of One (here philosophically hallucinated as Ego) and dyad (thought and being) by allowing the differences between the terms and their singular unrelated identities to be constitutive for thought. Rather than confusing thought and givenness, a modality of being in Marion, Laruelle claims that

> It suffices that the being of the Ego be given-one-time and be sufficiently consistent and autonomous that it does not necessitate that thought re-occurs to give a supplementary reality of consistency and closure, of system, to this duality. *There is* thought – *in order* to eventually think the Ego – but thought is not necessary – and perhaps even foreign – to the Ego itself which can be *given* without thought (of the "givenness") reviving it.[16]

In the remainder of this chapter we will examine what it would mean to think the Ego and thought as distinct from one another and how this opens up to Laruelle's conception of the force-(of)-thought.

HOW THE SUBJECT AND THE EGO ARE DIFFERENTIATED AND UNIFIED IN NON-PHILOSOPHY

In the previous section we looked at the ways in which the Ego and the subject have appeared in standard philosophy, highlighting first the importance of the subject in post-Kantian philosophy as the site upon which any epistemology has to be founded, before turning to the way the Ego has been confused with this subject through the Philosophical Decision found in Cartesian philosophy where the Ego unifies the split doublet of thought and being. In the remainder of the chapter, we will look at the way in which the subject and the Ego are thought under their unified theory in non-philosophy and the ways in which such a unified theory presents them in their identity or their immanence without a relation to one another. We will begin where we left off, with the Ego in non-philosophy, before turning to the theory of the subject present in the first name "force-(of)-thought."

Laruelle tells us that the task facing him is not an easy one:

> We have posted the following demand which we no longer know whether we can satisfy or not: to think the Real or the Ego as radically anterior to the subject of thought, determining it without being co-determined by it. Or moreover: to think the Ego such that it is neither thinkable nor unthinkable, form itself without relation to thought which is not without relation to the Ego. This demand has the effect of the very exclusion of the solution of Descartes or Henry, for whom thought remains *in spite of everything* co-determinant of the Ego, of its supposedly radical immanence. [...] If we must take account of thought, then in effect it must be about "thinking the Ego" and giving the Ego/thought duality; it is not necessary – if only philosophy demands it – that this *being-given* be once more a being-thought that that thought be redoubled or occur twice (as thought thought and thinking thought).[17]

In other words, the Ego is going to be found in non-philosophy as utterly distinct from thought, the force of which will be the subject. The Ego, which for our phenomenologists was the site of pure, undivided experience, has for the same phenomenologists also been confused as the being-given of a thought through the co-determination of the Ego and thought. Meaning, no thought, no thought of the Ego, and no Ego, no thought to be thought by a thinking thing. Instead of this redoubled sense of what it means to be given, Laruelle aims to give the Ego as simple radical immanence, foreclosed ultimately to thought, and without any kind of synthesis between thought and being (in this case, being as the modality of the being-given of the Ego). He writes, "Non-philosophy, giving itself the Ego as already manifested or as the Real, does not seek it, does not seek a subject/object synthesis as subject; it proceeds by cloning the transcendental identity that is the subject of the real identity of the Ego on one hand and on the other hand of philosophical materials. But real or simply transcendental, identity is never a synthesis."[18] That is, the identity of the Ego will be given in non-philosophy without any need for the Ego to be a site of synthesis.

While we know that Laruelle says the Ego will not be a synthesis, but an identity, what exactly does it mean to make such a claim? In order to get a handle on this, let's first skip ahead to Laruelle's theorem where he summarizes the place of the Ego in non-philosophy:

1 There is (the) Ego – but through the Ego itself.
2 The Ego is not – but (is) in-Ego and thus foreclosed to Being.
3 The Ego does not think – but gives itself as in-Ego and thus as foreclosed to thought.
Hence the theorem: *the Ego determines-in-the-last-instance, which is to say through transcendental cloning, the subject as force-(of)-thought.*[19]

Laruelle goes on to tell us that this theorem will be fully explained in the following chapter, where he focuses on determination-in-the-last-instance. Since this will be the focus of our next chapter as well, we can set aside that aspect of this description and the subsequent theorem and instead focus on the way Laruelle conceives of the identity of the Ego before looking at the identity of the subject. We see first that the Ego is said "to be" but only through itself. That is, the Ego is not dependent upon the doublet of thought/Being for its constitution, but has some irreducible identity that exists without relation. This requires the second statement, that the Ego is not or is "beyond Being" in the same way that the One and the Real are said to be beyond Being in Laruelle's work. They do not fit into an ontological circuit when the Ego is taken as rooted in nothing other than itself. This is clearly an abstract statement and it requires following the logic of radical immanence to make sense of it. That logic says that if the Ego is identity, and not a synthesis, then it is rooted in nothing other than itself and as rooted in nothing other than itself it cannot be said to "be" in any meaningful ontological sense. That is, the Ego is separated from one side of the doublet thought/Being.

The third statement removes the Ego from the other half of the doublet, thought. The Ego is said not to think, but is given, not thought, in-Ego. Laruelle often uses this syntax to refer to the givenness of something without remainder or excess. Therefore, to say that the Ego is given "in-Ego" is to repeat, in a manner, the preceding two statements. For it means that if the Ego is given as only from itself, that is without Being, then it is also given in a way that forecloses the Ego to thought. The Ego is not thought, but the modality of radical immanence that determines thought in-the-last-instance (the exact meaning of which will be explored in the next chapter). Such a point may appear materialist in character, though the reader should bear in mind that Laruelle would resist the forms of Philosophical Decision he thinks follow from materialism. Understanding that the system of materialism is under erasure here, Laruelle's point in seemingly less abstract language could be re-written to say something akin to: thought is dependent upon the living human being for its actuality. While the body may be thought in a kind of representational way, the fullness of its lived reality will remain unavailable to anything like a full thought. This is not, it is important to note, to say that we are unable to think reality, it is not a kind of skepticism or anti-rationalism, but simply the tracing of limits so as to delineate the ability of thought to model the lived without capturing it and to delineate the ways in which thought may hallucinate some kind of sufficiency in the face of this lived experience or Real.

In this conception of the Ego Laruelle follows the phenomenological tradition of Husserl and Henry in thinking the Ego as radical immanence, but he follows out the logic of this conception to think the Ego as a condition of thought, rather than the site of the unity of thought and Being. No such unity is sought, for there is no need for a kind of transcendental unity of thought and Being. Any such relation, even when it doesn't reach the level of a true unity, is dependent ultimately upon these two terms having an identity that structures such a relation in a transcendental manner, however abstract that may be. Laruelle sums this up in a whirlwind manner:

> The transcendental function does not modify the One or the Real, but it is inconceivable without it: *they are thus identical in vision-in-One*; the transcendental clone of the Ego is identity in-Ego. The transcendental One is therefore situated "between" the Real itself and an "empirical" given, here the abstract

and simple difference of thought and being, non-phenomenological Distance. Since in philosophy the difference between thought and being, which is neither one or the other, presents itself nonetheless as the work of thought itself, we will call the constituted structure of this transcendental identity a subject or *force-(of)-thought*, by its immediate relation to the "support" of universal and abstract Distance and of this vehicle itself. *It is the identity not of thought and being*, which would form a synthesis anew, *but-(of)-their abstract difference.*[20]

We see that the use of the terms One and Real are ultimately exchangeable depending upon the abstract context they are working in. We have already seen how the Ego and the One are also equivalent terms at differing intensities (the One being more abstract, it is able to be deployed in more powerful ways than the Ego for Laruelle). Thus we see that the Ego as One is given at a distance from thought and Being, which we know from our earlier discussion of Henry is always the shape of transcendence. However, for Laruelle this transcendence is not absolute, but relatively transcendental to the abstract difference of thought and being, rather than their unity or single identity. What does it mean to say relatively transcendental? It speaks ultimately to the ways in which thought and Being are cast as relationally dependent upon this unsplit Ego for their own identity in a way that the Ego is not dependent upon them. In this way the relative transcendental of the Ego is actually an immanence that signifies the Ego is not relational except in a unilateral way. That is, it is not a transcendence but a transcendental, or something that is given with the object as the condition for the appearance of that object.

This identification of the Ego's role allows us to begin to untangle the difference between the Ego and the subject in non-philosophy and how they may be unified but not turned into a confused unitary object. Laruelle summarizes this separation in a passage that we will first quote in its entirety and then unpack line by line in order to understand the identity he is presenting.

> Finally: a) the Ego does not think and is not a substance; the amphibology of the Ego and thought, of the Ego and being, is invalidated (if not dissolved). On the other hand, it is the "cause" not of thought and being but of the essence of their difference, a cause called "in-the-last-instance." Auto-reflection but also the semi-(re)flection of "auto-affection" are excluded from the Ego as Real, by definition it is foreclosed to thought; b) Thought is no longer a *res*, a substance, and still less an object, an essence, an end that the Ego would strive to achieve; rather from the outset it is "force" because it confuses itself with this non-phenomenological distance that unilaterally emerges from its transcendental essence. "Force" is a unilateral duality that carries out determination-in-the-last-instance and transcendental cloning for the first

56

time; c) The force-(of)-thought is the phenomenal content of the "subject." So much so that the Ego, purely immanent, neither objective nor subjective, can be accompanied but not necessarily by the subject of the force-(of)-thought. *The Ego and the subject cease to be confused and distinct at the heart of their sameness* [mêmeté]: *the Ego enjoys a radical autonomy, the subject a relative autonomy.* The amphibology of the philosophical expression "theory of the subject" is dissolved within an immanence of the Ego and a transcendence (but transcendental through its essence) of the subject as clone of the Ego.[21]

We see here that Laruelle thinks that this identification of the Ego and the subject as separate from one another dissolves the amphibology or confusing of identities of the Ego and the subject. This will be important, he claims, for the real theory of knowledge or knowing that will be developed in the next chapter. So, how is this separation carried out. He first says, "the Ego does not think and is not a substance; the amphibology of the Ego and thought, of the Ego and being, is invalidated (if not dissolved)." So we see that the Ego is no longer cast as the unity of thought and Being it was shown to be for Descartes and Hegel according to Marion. For the radical immanence of the Ego, discussed above as the Ego being rooted only itself, means that in order to think it we must think it without reference to thinking or Being. "On the other hand, it is the 'cause' not of thought and being but of the essence of their difference, a cause called 'in-the-last-instance'." Here Laruelle claims that the radical immanence of the Ego is the "cause" "in-the-last-instance" of the difference of thought and Being, that rather than the Ego being the unity of their difference, it is in some way productive of the very difference between thought and Being. Both Being and thought are ultimately separate from the Ego but in ways that are different, and that difference in non-relation is touched on as Laruelle continues.

"Thought is no longer a *res*, a substance, and still less an object, an essence, an end that the Ego would strive to achieve; rather from the outset it is 'force' because it confuses itself with this non-phenomenological distance that unilaterally emerges from its transcendental essence." So thought cannot relate to the Ego as a being (a general name for the *res* [thing], substance, object, essence, or end, which Laruelle lists), but instead emerges as something akin to "force" in the distance between the Ego's immanence and its transcendental essence. As an example, try imagining yourself. In that moment of thinking yourself your thought is different from who you are in ways you cannot bring to thought (including all of the biological processes going on, all the psychological history that makes you the kind of person who would want to pick up this book, the socio-economic background that has allowed you to have the education and the time to engage with such a book, and a million other seemingly disparate things), and yet such a thought of your self only emerges from the radical immanence or irreducible identity of yourself. "'Force' is a unilateral duality that carries out determination-in-the-last-instance and transcendental cloning for the first time." Laruelle's use of "force" should not be confused with something akin to a violent forcing. Force, and particularly "force-(of)-thought," is here related to the French *force de travail* or "force of work" that is more familiar to us in English as "labor power." So to claim that "thought is a force" is to claim that it does something, produces something, in the same way that labor power produces new objects in the world. So, thought is no longer a thing, but now something that human bodies can do, something that may effect the very concepts and first names Laruelle has put into play.

"The force-(of)-thought is the phenomenal content of the 'subject'." Here Laruelle brings us to his identification of the subject. The Ego, we have already seen, names a radical immanence that is utterly distinct from thought and Being as transcendentals that would structure this immanence (for such structuring would contravene immanence), but the subject has some special relationship to thought. The subject, as in standard philosophy, has a special relationship to thought, but not as a mediating site. Instead the force-(of)-thought is how the subject "appears," the subject as thinking thing is only a force-(of)-thought or the very power which thinking is. However, this real subject and phenomenal appearance as force-(of)-thought cannot be the Ego because, as Laruelle says, it is the phenomenal appearance of the subject. "So much so that the Ego, purely immanent, neither objective nor subjective, can be accompanied but not necessarily by the subject of the force-(of)-thought." The Ego is not an object or a subject, but radical immanence, the subject is a "clone" of the Ego (we will deal with what Laruelle means by this term in Chapter 4), thus is related but different, meaning that the subject is indeed dependent upon the Ego for its own identity, which is the meaning behind Laruelle's statement that "*The Ego and the subject cease to be confused and distinct at the heart of their sameness* [mêmeté]: *the Ego enjoys a radical autonomy, the subject a relative autonomy.*" This relationship between radical and relative autonomy will become clearer in the next chapter, as it is at the heart of the meaning of determination-in-the-last-instance.

THE FORCE-(OF)-THOUGHT AS CORRECTIVE TO DEFLATIONARY AND NOSTALGIC ACCOUNTS OF THE HUMAN SUBJECT

All of this should help the reader to unpack Laruelle's argument and situate it within wider standard philosophical concerns and discussions around the Ego and the subject. However, the reader may still be wondering what exactly is at stake in Laruelle's identification and differentiation of the Ego and the subject. As we noted at the beginning of the chapter, most of contemporary European philosophy has been split between, on the one hand, some form of thought that reduces everything to how it may be thought or represented rationally as what something "really is," and, on the other hand, a form of philosophy that seeks to protect in some sense the unity of experience, the dignity of those elements of life that either cannot be captured by rationality alone or that are severely impoverished when thought only according to rationalistic and scientific means. There are, from both Laruelle's perspective and my own, reasons and affects that support both positions. But neither position can really claim to account for the lived reality of the human being, which includes both thinking and feeling, acting and being acted upon, and a multiplicity of other functions and aspects of human life. In Laruelle's non-philosophy, philosophy and science are not abstract regimes of knowledge production that require human beings to submit to them and be formed by them; science and philosophy are instead created for human beings. Thus, the goal of separating out the Ego and the subject is to clarify the ways in which philosophy both may be used by human beings and how the Real of the human is foreclosed to philosophical knowledge.

The aspect of Laruelle's thought that axiomatically claims the Real of the human is foreclosed is something akin to an escape route from the false choice between deflationary or nostalgic accounts of what the human being is, i.e. those accounts that either reduce the human to being "just" a body (as if a body were ever "just" anything) or nostalgically cast the human being as having some authentic essence. Both are forms of philosophical authoritarianism and can be the philosophical support for truly horrific political and ethical acts, or a thousand small acts carried out each day. But since Laruelle's conception of the Ego as a kind of modality of the One or the Real is developed in part from his engagement with phenomenologists like Henry, it may appear to take on the same problems of idealism that haunt Henry's conception of the auto-affection that forms the basis of philosophical knowledge. While auto-affection is an important concept in Henry's phenomenology, going as far back as his earliest major work, *Essence of Manifestation*, the idealist character of auto-affection that Laruelle claims haunts Henry's conception of radical immanence is most clearly seen in his discussion of life as found in *I Am the Truth*. There Henry writes: "Life designates a pure manifestation, always irreducible to that of the world, an original revelation that is not the revelation of an other thing and does not depend on anything other, but is rather a revelation of self, that absolute self-revelation that is Life itself."[22] Here life takes on the general character of the Ego already discussed, since both are for Henry

a "pure manifestation [...] irreducible to the world," or that field of rela-
tionality that would code over the reality of life in the name of something
other than life, reducing it to biology or some other "science" (a negative
term for Henry, but not for Laruelle). Where Henry begins to stray into
an idealist conception of modalities of the One, like the Ego or life (which
Laruelle will refer to as the lived-without-life to disempower this idealism),
is by always thinking auto-affectivity rather than the Ego or life as such.
Consider Henry's claim that "What is specific to life is, in effect, that it
affects itself. This auto-affection defines its living; the 'experiencing-itself'
of which it consists."[23] Laruelle tells us that auto-affection "confuses
itself in reality with cognitive immediacy or immediacy from the Ego to
thought," meaning that ultimately the radical immanence of the Ego or the
lived-without-life (or simply Life in Henry's terms) is confused with one
of its form of relations, this time its immediate relation to itself.[24]

Such a philosophy of immediacy is not, however, simply an anti-
reductionism in the service of some religious or theological project, despite
Henry's own constant theological references from *Essence of Manifestation*
to his explicitly theological later works. While the theological turn has
often been read as a rejection of science, and Henry is perhaps the most
explicitly anti-scientistic thinker in French phenomenology, it does not
engage in some kind of "barbarous" irrationalism. Henry thinks a theory
of knowledge can be developed from this position and even writes, "*Truth
and affection are equivalent terms.*"[25] Thus this conception of auto-affection
is, for Henry, an epistemology, but one that is utterly distinct from and
unintelligible to the "Galilean sciences," which is his term for all the
sciences after Galileo that reduce phenomena to something other than their
fullness and deprive the self of its immediacy, thus losing the very basis of
knowledge.[26] The force-(of)-thought may appear to a reader familiar with
Henry to mimic auto-affection, since both appear to be a kind of action
that issues from something with a special relationship to the term radical
immanence (the One, the Ego, life, etc.). That Laruelle takes the time to
recognize and refute such a suggestion suggests that auto-affection is a
kind of philosophical form of force-(of)-thought and influential in his own
working up of the concept. However, there is a major difference between
force-(of)-thought and auto-affection summarized by Laruelle as follows:
"Auto-affection is in one case assumed to be already the very content of the
Ego, which is thereby reduced, while in the other the force-(of)-thought
infers itself from the Ego which determines it."[27] Laruelle rejects the overdetermining nature of the focus on immediacy in Henry's epistemology (as
well as rejecting his anti-science extremist stance). The unified theory of
philosophy and science as a non-philosophical epistemology proposed by
Laruelle is not a philosophy of immediacy; his recognition of something

like the Ego underlying knowledge in phenomenology is a recognition of a philosophical projection of the One that leads to a confusion, either through immediacy or a reductive mediation, of the One with philosophy's im/mediations.

So against the kind of nostalgic protection of a hallucinated and idealist essence of the human as auto-affective life, Laruelle instead posits a radical immanence of the Ego as modality of the One or the Real which is foreclosed to thought. Thus, the failure of these sorts of philosophies is explained in part through the argument of *Principles of Non-Philosophy* as the failure to stop confusing some effect of this radical immanence, like the subject as force-(of)-thought, with the Ego itself. Instead of focusing upon the impossibility of a theory of the Ego, Laruelle posits the foreclosed nature of the Ego as a kind of axiom that is operative but not the object or subject of a knowledge or the act of knowing. This will take us in the next chapter to a theory of the subject as force-(of)-thought explained by determination-in-the-last-instance. Instead of the subject as force-(of)-thought being something akin to the "I" or the Ego, we will see there that "the 'subject' or force-(of)-thought is the complex phenomenal content of what philosophy redoubles or hallucinates as 'Other'."[28] Thus, in the next chapter, we will begin to look at the question of Otherness or Alterity in non-philosophy as it relates to the One.

4

Unilateral Causality and the Pragmatic Theory of Philosophy

Moving from Chapter 3, "Unified or 'Non-Cartesian' Theory of the Subject," to Chapter 4, "Determination-in-the-last-instance," the reader may feel a certain sense of exasperation at the abjectly abstract quality of the later chapter. While many philosophers are often difficult to follow owing to their abstraction, they claim that abstraction to be in some sense a reflection of concrete reality, explaining how things "really are" (metaphysics), or at least how things "really should be" (ethics). Non-Philosophy's abstraction, however, does not claim to provide a comprehensive overview of reality, or rather of the Real foreclosed to that reality, but instead aims at something closer to a pragmatics of thought. That is, non-philosophy's abstraction arises from its being a theory of philosophy and not a theory of the Real. In an interview, Laruelle describes the abstraction of non-philosophy as a second order abstraction: "Philosophy is very abstract, by definition, but it is an abstraction closer to the concrete; this is the first degree of abstraction. As non-philosophy is a theory of philosophy, we have an abstraction in the second degree."[1] But, the reader may ask, well within his or her rights, why would one take up the arduous task of working through such abstraction? What is it that non-philosophy promises us, especially here in one of its most abstract forms as the development of its fundamental principles, concepts, and method?

The answer is largely implicit throughout *Principles of Non-Philosophy*, although Laruelle explicitly focuses on such a question in his other works, like *Future Christ* and *Struggle and Utopia at the End Times of Philosophy*, where the focus is on questions of human suffering and salvation worked out through Judeo-Christian religious materials in a non-religious, non-Christian register (in the sense that Laruelle intends the "non"). However, towards the end of Chapter 4, "Determination-in-the-last-instance," Laruelle provides us with a vision of the soteriological function of non-philosophy in relation to the abject abstraction of his development of the causality of determination-in-the-last-instance:

> The operation of force "over" resistance makes non-philosophy, rather than a "pragmatic history of the human spirit" (Fichte), a *pragmatic theory of philosophy in terms of man as last-instance*. Non-Philosophy or whatever unified theory it renders possible is a theory rather than a history, a theory infinitely opened by the contingency of the given and by the unilateralization carried out by the force-(of)-thought rather than a history circularly accomplishing itself in the synthesis or 'philosophical' reconciliation of the contraries of the I and the non-I, of philosophy and collective consciousness, albeit in a non substantial manner and in an infinite effort of realization of self. Non-Philosophy thus re-opens history by liberating it from its philosophical enclosure.[2]

A number of the terms here will be the focus of our engagement in this chapter: the I and the non-I and their non-philosophical mutations as One and non(-One), resistance, unilateralization and its relation to the concept of cloning. For now, however, let us focus on the relation of Fichte's famously enigmatic description of his "science of knowing" (*Wissenschaftslehre*) as a "pragmatic history of the human spirit" to Laruelle's own mutational gloss on this description describing non-philosophy as a "pragmatic theory of philosophy in terms of man as last-instance." Fichte's project of a *Wissenschaftslehre* or science of knowing was an early and major contribution to German Idealism that eventually both Schelling and Hegel rejected and contrasted their own philosophies with. Fichte's description of his project prefigures Laruelle's description of non-philosophy, but Fichte's description is also prefigured since his conception of a pragmatic history is likely borrowed from Salomon Maimon's own conception of a pragmatic history of philosophy that would not be an empirical history, but an a priori history, looking at the ways in which a philosophical concept "had to be determined" as it exists outside the individual philosophers.[3] For Fichte the purpose of such an a priori or pragmatic history (the two terms are related in both Maimon, Fichte, and Laruelle) is to ground philosophical reflection upon an act or action rather than upon an idea. Non-Philosophy continues in this tradition, however heretically, by emphasizing itself as a *theory* of philosophy in a way that Fichte's focus on the history of concepts and philosophy does not. While both aim to provide an understanding of philosophy and its ground, non-philosophy is more explicit about liberating the human being and what "history" may be in a non-philosophical register. Laruelle's sense of the pragmatic may be seen to share much in common with Kant's definition when he defines it in his *Anthropology from a Pragmatic Perspective* as "what man, considered as a freely active being, makes of himself or what he can and should make of himself."[4]

Non-Philosophy is a theory of philosophy, not of the World or the objects which philosophy claims to bring before its own gaze, but a theory of philosophy itself as a structure overdetermining thought and practice. The promise of non-philosophy, then, is not so much for a free human being to make something of him or herself, but to make something of philosophy for human use without philosophy turning into a golem.

The reader may therefore find their frustration at the abject abstraction of Chapter 4 is reduced when they recognize its object is philosophy and not the World. The previous chapter focused on the philosophical thematic of the subject and the Ego, with the subject being cast as the force-(of)-thought. This meant that you, the reader, are not the subject. The primary identity of human beings is not as a subject, but rather the subject is a projection from the One (explained through the modality of the Ego). In so far as you are a subject or there is a force-(of)-thought, it is because you have some identity in-One, irreducible to or in a non-relation to the subject. The purpose of Chapter 4 is to develop the conditions for this non-philosophical claim. As with the previous chapter, there is a philosophical forerunner to the non-philosophical determination-in-the-last-instance (hereafter abbreviated as DLI), in this case it is the thematic of causality as conditioning or determining. Laruelle tells us that DLI is a specific causality: "non-philosophy has a specific causality allowing it to eliminate formalism and idealism, materialism, teleology and technologism."[5] But this causality requires philosophy as material, precisely those philosophies that DLI eliminates in terms of their self-sufficiency. So again, we see here that non-philosophy will refuse the usual taking up of some philosophical position in favor of developing a theory of philosophy that takes philosophy as its object to be known and its material for building with.

This chapter will help orient the reader of Laruelle's text in a slightly different manner than the preceding ones. Rather than focusing on providing the philosophical background to this chapter, we will instead trace the constellation of terms and expand on these terms. This is in line with our goal of providing a constellation and not a totalizing map of the territory. It will help orient the reader as they travel through the original text where a number of important arguments will be made in a tangential way (in the geometric sense and not a pejorative one), arguments that will not be fully explicated here. While providing a short description of DLI, we will then turn to the way it is expressed in a kind of formalism as the interplay between the (non-)One, non(-One), and One-in-One. This will then lead us to a discussion of resistance as centered on the term of the non(-One). This in turn leads us to a discussion of Laruelle's seemingly enigmatic concept of cloning that ultimately we will come to see more clearly when we recognize that it is a non-philosophical mutation of philosophy's obsession with speculation and the attendant concepts of mirror and reflection.

FROM PHILOSOPHICAL MATERIALS TO NON-PHILOSOPHICAL SYNTAX

At the start of this chapter Laruelle signals to us that the preceding chapter had been concerned in some sense with the materials of a unified theory (the philosophies of the subject and the Ego) and he now marks the present chapter as concerned with elucidating the syntax of the unified theory of philosophy and science.[6] In other words, this chapter has to do with the ways in which the material of language is arranged, how the material itself relates. In so far as non-philosophy is an abstraction of philosophy's abstraction, and so a second-order abstraction, then the syntax of DLI elucidated in *Principles of Non-Philosophy* concerns the way we speak about the relationship between the Real (or the One, again they are equivalent terms) and its effects, a relationship that Laruelle refers to as "delicate."[7] So what makes that relationship delicate? While remembering the directive that non-philosophy does what it says and says what it does, we can recognize that part of what is delicate in this relationship is our own description of it, since it too is subject to syntax. From the perspective of non-philosophy this means that our description is subject to a standard philosophical syntax that also bashes through the delicate lines of relation and leads to a confusion of the Real with its effects. The non-philosophical syntax outlined here is an attempt to think delicately, what in Laruelle's current work he would refer to as thinking at the level of the quantum rather than at the level of macro objects.[8]

It is important to understand that in non-philosophy the Real or the One precedes Being and representation and that in fact these macro, metaphysical objects are effects of the Real or the One.[9] This is a familiar thesis to readers of Neoplatonism and the form of this argument may even be seen to some extent in Emmanuel Levinas' thesis that the question of alterity or otherness (ethics) precedes the question of Being (ontology).[10] Following Laruelle's suggestion that the standard philosophical theme of the Other or Alterity is mutated in the thinking of DLI, it is not surprising to see that this mutation finds its material in a standard philosophical thesis. That this material may be found in both Greek Neoplatonism and in the challenge to the "Greek" (i.e. European) obsession with the question of Being present in Levinas' bringing to bear of the Jewish tradition upon non-Jewish philosophy speaks to its need for a radicalization so as to overcome its amphibology.[11] What separates Laruelle's understanding of the causality of the One from Neoplatonism is that he is not concerned with the question of emanation or procession, or how effects like Being flow from the One, but rather with what he calls "precession" (*précession*). That is, what is at play is the radical autonomy or "scission" of the One that precedes and cuts off the effect from reversing the causality and effecting the One. While in Neoplatonism, especially as taken up by Christian thinkers in the Middle Ages, there is a relationship of *exitus et reditus*, or the exit of the effects from the transcendent One that then return to the transcendent One, within non-philosophy we may say that nothing ever exits from the One and so has nothing to return to. Instead the essence of the One is utterly indifferent to its effects and does not even act upon its effects, but instead only in so far as thinking and being (and alterity and other effects) are "in-One" does the One even act. That is, only in so far as "in-the-last-instance" all effects are in-One does the One itself even act, since action is also an effect of the One.

This description of the One resists representation and thus also resists being explained by recourse to something other than itself, i.e. it literally resists being re-presented. But it is not an arbitrary description, instead flowing from what is implied in the conception of radical immanence that in part drives the project of non-philosophy. As Laruelle explains, "Since radical immanence remains by definition in itself, it cannot move out of itself or produce something like Being or moreover beings, [radical immanence] will be a 'negative' but universal condition."[12] A negative condition but one that is universal refers to a condition that does nothing, but to which everything deployed within philosophy (Being, beings, alterity, and so on) is related. The causality of immanence then provides the material for which Laruelle rethinks the causality of DLI or unilateral causality, which form equivalent terms in his work: "Unilateral causality is not an *ex nihilo* invention of non-philosophy. Its usage in terms of radical immanence, rather, is a theoretical discovery which itself has a history, foundational for non-philosophy."[13] He summarizes that history by locating what he calls the classical axiom: "The classical axiom of the philosophical usage of unilaterality is as follows: *the effect distinguishes itself from the cause which does not distinguish itself from it.*"[14] This description of unilateral causality equates it ultimately with what medieval philosophers and theologians called the immanent cause and which, through the influence of Duns Scotus and the independent development of the idea undertaken by Spinoza, was taken up by contemporary thinkers like Heidegger and Deleuze. Daniel W. Smith, writing about Deleuze's conception of univocity, summarizes the immanent cause using language that is independent from Laruelle's but whose similarity may help readers of Laruelle begin to grasp his meaning: "An *immanent* cause, finally, is a cause that not only remains within itself in order to produce, but one whose produced effect also remains within it."[15] Laruelle spends much of the section "On Causality as 'Unilateral Duality'" distinguishing the "ambiguous or imprecise" formula of the classical axiom from the non-philosophical usage of it, but the difference ultimately lies in the way an immanent cause is understood in philosophy to create a circle and the way in which non-philosophy breaks that circularity. In the standard philosophical use of the classical axiom, as in Deleuze's philosophy, immanence is immanence to something else whether that be Being or beings or alterity; in short immanence is immanent to its effects. Laruelle arguably takes more seriously the notion that the produced effect remains within the cause (the One) since in-the-last-instance Being or Otherness will be in-One, but he goes further in arguing that this means the only thing the One is immanent to is itself. Graphically this is communicated by suspending the relation's third term: the One is immanent (to) itself.[16]

With this difference between the standard and non-standard philosophical uses of the classical axiom clear, we may now sketch out the shape of DLI and the related concept of unilateral duality. First, let us look outside of *Principles of Non-Philosophy* to Laruelle's *Introduction to Non-Marxism* where we also find a chapter-long explication of DLI, and then fill out this explication with the importance of radical and relative autonomy in *Principles of Non-Philosophy*. In *Introduction to Non-Marxism*, instead of speaking of the One and its effects, he speaks simply and more schematically with reference to the One and the Two (so the One and an effect, like Being). He writes, "it is not matter of 'difference,' of the co-extension of the One and the Two, of the One that is Two and of the Two which is One in some reversible way. It seems, instead, that DLI must be irreversible, the One is only One, even with the Two, and the Two forms a Two with the One only from its point of view as the Two."[17] This is a reiteration of the thesis of radical immanence from the perspective of causality. The One or the Real is only immanent (to) itself and so anything that may be called an effect of it is only ever a kind of projection or what Laruelle will often refer to as an "objective appearance." The meaning of this term is actually clear when we begin to understand the status of the effects of the Real. When Laruelle lays out the conditions or terms according to which we can locate the unilateral duality of the One-Real and its effects he does so with reference to the status of autonomy and the modifiers radical and relative.[18] So an objective appearance may be understood as a way of speaking both to the autonomy of an effect of the Real – for example "the world of beings" or even "the face of the Other" (to pick a Heideggerian and a Levinasian example) – as well as to the status of this autonomy as relative since in-the-last-instance this effect is only a Two in relation to the One.

The One retains a radical autonomy from its effects and so is not alienated in having effects or objects and does not require or even inspire any kind of longing of return in those effects and objects. In fact, as we will see later in this chapter, the radical autonomy of the One elicits resistance in its effects, despite the One's indifference to that resistance (since in-the-last-instance resistance too is in-One).

At this point it is important to reiterate that Laruelle's description here is one of philosophy's inner working, that he is not making an argument about the metaphysics of reality, but instead tracing the structure of philosophy. So there is no "One" in a metaphysical sense, but rather this name operates pragmatically within philosophy. However, this does not mean that Laruelle is a relativist in some naive, philosophical sense. Nor is his work an example of linguistic idealism. He may be read as a realist, albeit and unsurprisingly in a non-standard sense. As we saw above in more detail, DLI implies a relative autonomy of a given = X that the One or the Real effectuates. Within the names that populate philosophy this X may be Being or beings or the Other, but Laruelle also claims that other forms of knowing or knowledge are subject to the same effectuation of some One or Real, so this given = X may also be one of the names that are important within other regional forms of knowing, like God within religion or the crime against humanity within ethics. And ultimately, this relatively autonomous X "ends up drawing its ultimate sense from the One in so far as it is by remaining in itself: this is a 'realism' of-the-last-instance, or rather a real-without-realism, not an absolute idealism."[19] Without returning to the elucidation in Chapter 2 of this book, we can note that this realism is taken by Laruelle from the way science, at the level of *practice* and prior to any spontaneous philosophy that may be found outside that practice, relates to the Real without metaphysical overdetermination. In so far as science also has a theoretical or spontaneously philosophical element, those names may also be subject to this non-philosophical posture.

SCHEMATISM OF THE ONE

In the preceding section we looked at the way DLI and unilateral duality provide different forms of syntax for non-philosophy. This syntax, sometimes referred to as unitax by Laruelle (with some humor implied) to emphasize the unilateral rather than synthetic character of non-philosophy, provides the framework for how one goes about working with philosophical materials as well as materials derived from other regional forms of knowing. That is, syntax is about how one goes about doing and saying something with regard to philosophy's own internal syntax that it casts as transcendental to itself. The internal syntax of non-philosophy is also known as the structure of the Philosophical Decision, a concept that we are not explicating here since it was the focus of much of the original Anglophone reception of Laruelle. In *Principles of Non-Philosophy* the syntax of Philosophical Decision is summarized as a matrix "in fractional or semi-real 2/3 terms" whereas non-philosophy presents "a simpler matrix, in two real 'terms' + one transcendental term."[20] The fact that philosophy is presented here as fractional speaks to the way philosophy's syntax always tends towards some kind of system of unity that it thinks reflects and co-determines the Real or One of the fraction, but in fact simply reflects the fractured philosophical syntax itself. So, for example, in the classic question of how thinking and being come together, philosophy first separates them into two distinct things (the 2 in the 2/3); the task then is to search for something to unite them, some third term of synthesis – the 3 in the 2/3 which is the first two terms repeated with a synthesizing third term. This third term is often an enlarged or "transcendentalized" version of one of the first two, so that idealism presents the synthesis as a matter of a thinking of thought and being whereas materialism unites thinking and being by grounding them both in matter, which is one way Being is said.

Getting to grips with Laruelle's conception of the Philosophical Decision is often difficult, but the difficulty may be alleviated if the reader understands that it is an attempt to trace a general structure found in philosophy and so is necessarily abstract. If Laruelle's modeling of philosophy's structure is correct, then it follows that readers should be able to locate it at play in standard philosophy and fill out the skeleton structure with the terminological skin particular to that philosophy. This is indeed the task Laruelle works out in *Philosophies of Difference* where the theory of Philosophical Decision is formulated most clearly, whereas in *Principles of Non-Philosophy* we are shown how to use the non-philosophical syntax to *make use* of the terms located within standard philosophical decisions. First, non-philosophy treats the first two terms of the philosophical fraction as a unilateral duality within a wider structure of DLI where this unilateral duality itself is only unilaterally related to the One. This allows us to see the amphibology or reversibility of the terms that philosophy hallucinates as the Real itself. For example, instead of pitching idealism or materialism against one another, we see the ways in which the relationship between thinking and being may be unilateralized producing different effects; speaking very summarily, thinking and being may only be a duality from the perspective of thought which is dependent on being or from the perspective of being since being is carried in thought. The debate and difference between these two philosophical positions is disempowered by the non-philosophical posture of taking these unilateral dualities as in-the-last-instance in-One. Or, in other terms, the various ways a unilateral duality may be cast are shown to rely ultimately upon a greater unilateral duality of the One and its effects. This means that the One or the Real is never touched by non-philosophy. Unlike philosophy, non-philosophy does not envelop or englobe its terms into a world or thought-world it takes as the Real. Instead these terms are treated as local and material.

Since the working out of non-philosophy is immanent to non-philosophy's practice, we see in this chapter Laruelle making use of a specific philosophical syntax in his own development of the syntax of non-philosophy. That syntax is lifted from Fichte's *Wissenschaftslehre* or *Science of Knowledge*. By looking to how Laruelle takes and recasts this philosophical syntax we will be able both to delineate a schematic of the One and see how he himself makes use of philosophical material by way of the syntax of non-philosophy. That is, we will see that non-philosophy says what it does and does what it says, as Laruelle puts it in distinction to philosophy.[21] So what exactly does non-philosophy say about the One? Returning to the distinction between the 2/3 terms of philosophy and the two real terms + one transcendental term of non-philosophy we see that these two real terms can be abstractly mapped onto three different ways of writing, or graphemes of, the One. The two "real terms" are written more abstractly as the One or (non-)One (though this use is rare) and the non(-One). The transcendental term is written abstractly as the One-in-One. However, as you read what follows below, it is important to keep in mind that Laruelle's claim is not about a metaphysical One or a unity. The non-philosophical conception of the One is not an instance of metaphysics, "The non-philosophical conception of the real-One [...] is not the Whole."[22] It is an abstraction of philosophy's functioning.

The schematism takes two axioms and a theorem of non-philosophy and compares and differentiates them with three of the guiding principles of Fichte's project. We have grouped them together first so that the reader may start by considering them together before we take them one by one in order to elucidate the schematism of the One:

Axiom 1: The One is the One-in-One; or moreover: The One is not but is-in-one or "vision-in-one." In other words: the I is I-in-I.
Wissenschaftslehre 1st principle: I = I.[23]

Axiom 2: There is a non(-One) or a resistance to the One.
Wissenschaftslehre 2nd principle: a non-I is opposed to I.[24]

Theorem: The One-in-One is the identity-in-the-last-instance of the unilateral duality of the indivisible One and the divisible *and* indivisible non(-One);

this identity is the organon of thought or force-(of)-thought, as solution to the problem of the determination of the non(-One) by the One.
Wissenschaftslehre, 3rd principle: I oppose in the I, to the divisible I, a divisible non-I.[25]

As each term is mapped onto Fichte's project the reader may wonder what exactly it is that Fichte's philosophy does that makes it so valuable to Laruelle. Laruelle describes Fichte's work as "one of the most lucid positions, one of the most beautiful solutions to the problem of philosophy."[26] The problem of philosophy as Fichte understood it was to "furnish the ground of all experience."[27] For Laruelle this has to do with the way philosophy structures what he calls our hallucination of the World as englobing and structuring the Human in its radical immanence, or the Human-in-Human (and the ungendered nature of the possessive pronoun "its" is intentional).[28] And in a certain sense this too is what Fichte meant as he aimed to trace the a priori structure of experience that appears simply to just be:

> the question, "What is the source of the system of presentations which are accompanied by the feeling of necessity, and of this feeling of necessity itself?" is one that is surely worthy of reflection. It is the task of philosophy to provide an answer to this question, and in my opinion nothing is philosophy save the science which performs this task. The system of presentations accompanied by the feeling of necessity is also called *experience*, both internal and external.[29]

If Fichte's system is beautiful as a philosophy it still ultimately roots this philosophical structure not in the World or in philosophy, but in the radical identity of the I, much the way Laruelle sees the science of non-philosophy as being concerned with the question of the defense of the radically immanent Human rooted in a Human that philosophy does not know since it always submits the Human to something other than it.[30] Again, we see that non-philosophy aims to be "*a pragmatic theory of philosophy in terms of man as last-instance*" but is not a neo-Fichteanism.[31]

ONE-IN-ONE

To see how Laruelle's non-philosophy differs from a neo-Fichteanism we have to first understand what Fichte was doing. Fichte named his project a "transcendental idealism" which sought to ground our experience in a transcendental and unitary I, rather than grounding experience in a mix of self (I) and what lies outside it, the so-called "real world," or in Kantian terms what could be called the world of appearances. While this would appear to suggest that Fichte is an idealist of the kind that common sense leads others to mock, i.e. an idealist who denies the existence of the outside world, his project is far more subtle and rooted in a rejection of a certain obfuscatory power in Kant's philosophy with regard to the inaccessibility of the "in-itself" reality of things. Specifically, Fichte rejects the distinction between the realms of the noumenal (the thing-in-itself, ultimately inaccessible to human experience) and the phenomenal (the realm of how things appear and are experienced by a subject). It is this distinction that ultimately leads Kant to distinguish between the realms of pure or theoretical reason (related to mathematics and the reason deployed in abstract intellectual work) and practical reason (related to action in the world, or more abstractly to ethics and politics). This not only invites a certain skepticism in terms of action in the social realm, but also gives us a split image of the human person which for Fichte leads only to skepticism and dogmatism.

As Frederick Neuhouser summarizes it in his summary of Fichte's philosophy *as* a philosophy of subjectivity:

> the most important way in which Fichte's own theory of subjectivity aimed to improve upon Kant's was by providing a *unitary* account of the subject, one that would bring "unity and coherence into the human being" by showing that there are not two distinct faculties of reason but, at root, only one. His task, then, takes the form of a search to discover the single principle that governs the entire realm of subjectivity [and thereby experience, since this is united in the human being] – a principle that defines what it is to be a subject in a theoretical as well as a practical sense.[32]

As Fichte sees it, the only way to avoid these two traps is to find a way to ground experience in a phenomenon that is unitary (undivided) and absolute (indubitable). This cannot be the outside world, because in Kant's philosophy we only have knowledge of the outside world or external ground of our existence though an inference about causality. As Fichte writes,

> How broadly, then, according to *Kant*, does the applicability of all the categories extend, and in particular that of causality? Only over the realm of appearances; and thus only over what is already for us and in us. And how, then, could one arrive at the assumption of a something distinct from the self, as a ground of the empirical content of knowledge? Only, I take it, by an inference from the grounded to the ground; hence, by application of the concept of causality.[33]

Thus, instead of accepting a distinction between noumenal and phenomenal and then rejecting the external world as the ground for knowledge, Fichte instead posits the absolute identity of the I or self (the French translate Fichte's *Ich* as *Moi* while English translations use I). This is the meaning of the philosophical equation I = I.[34] The ground of experience is absolute in its simplicity and abstraction. Like Descartes' cogito the I = I is grounded in a kind of absolutely certain experience, but unlike the cogito it retains a simplicity and unity that isn't split between thinking and being.

This abstract simplicity is part of what Laruelle takes up in his thinking of the One-in-One, which he also is willing to equate with the I-in-I. This equivocation tells us that Laruelle's non-philosophy is grounded not on something exterior to the I, but upon a radicalized version of the I or Human-in-Human. While Laruelle is adamant that this is a kind of philosophy or thinking of the real-without-realism, it does mean that non-philosophy is in large part unconcerned with an empirical or historical theory of philosophy. For Laruelle, a science of philosophy, like his non-philosophy, has to arise out of the abstraction of philosophy itself. It cannot mark itself as absolutely distinct from that philosophy without falling into a kind of "spontaneous philosophy" hidden within it. Yet, despite this equivocation, Laruelle still insists on thinking the I-in-I though the austere abstraction of the One-in-One.

This commitment to abstraction is what marks the real distinction between Fichte and Laruelle regarding identity. Fichte's I = I is an example of his attempt to ground his transcendental philosophy in the I alone, with knowledge of this grounding being given through the Kantian concept of intellectual intuition. While in Kant's philosophy certain forms of intuition are generally endorsed, like the "pure intuitions" of space and time, these tend to be intuitions based in the empirical rather than transcendental realm.[35] Intuitions of the intellectual sort refer to transcendental elements of experience and so they are, for Kant, necessarily limited to objects that are not sensible, but symbolic or discursive (as in pure mathematics).[36] Historically, the theological sense of divine intellectual intuition was that the divine knowing and creating of the object are the same thing, and in some sense this form of intuition can be seen in certain considerations of pure mathematics. This form of intellectual intuition is rejected by Kant's boundary-marking epistemology and it is not this form of intellectual intuition that Fichte picks up. In the most general terms intellectual intuition refers to a way of knowing where "the subject's intuiting activity is, in some sense, indistinguishable from the object of intuition."[37] For Fichte intellectual intuition is able to be applied to the subject or I because of the apperception of the existence of the I carried in all other knowledge. This description of apperception is taken directly from Kant in his discussion of the "I think."[38] But Fichte ultimately is dissatisfied with the distinction between sensible and conceptual intuition as part and parcel of the split between the noumenal and phenomenal already rejected by Fichte as it rends the subject in two.

Much of this will look like Laruelle's project already. After all, there is in Laruelle an intentional collapsing of philosophical dualisms through the causality of unilateral duality. Much of his critique is precisely about the decisions, or splittings, that operate in philosophy and create a certain kind of thought-world that endlessly harasses the human. Ultimately, however, intellectual intuition still carries out the structure of philosophical decision in subordinating identity (the being of the I) to intellect (the thinking of the I as equal to I), such that the being and the thinking of that being are simultaneous. Laruelle explains the difference: "What distinguishes the I-in-I and the I = I, two forms of the identity of the I? In spite of the variation of its significations or usages in Fichte, I = I remains an intellectual intuition in the most general sense of the term whereas the I-in-I is a non-intuitive identity, and real rather than logical or maintaining a last relation to logic."[39] Rather than marking a difference between the I, marked by the transcendental arithmetic of the equals sign, Laruelle's I-in-I or One-in-One is described as a non-intellectual identity. This is an identity that is foreclosed to thinking and being altogether in its pure abstraction, and so it is real in this way as beyond or, more accurately, preceding the philosophical doublet of thinking and being altogether. As the One-in-One is then not an intellectual intuition, it is not the same thing as the apperception of the I in all other thinking. In many ways it is an unthinkable notion in any straightforward, common sense way. Yet Laruelle's claim is that this expresses axiomatically the Real that precedes thought and being, that precedes the Ego and the subject, but is also another name for radical human immanence. In a certain sense, as he writes, it is a transcendental term that is used to recognize and think otherwise with the various forms of the Philosophical Decision.

On this point there may be a certain confusion over the terminological choice of "transcendental" to describe the One-in-One when the One-in-One is also referred to as being radically immanent to itself. The common post-Kantian differentiation between a transcendent term or transcendence, a transcendental, and an immanent term or immanence should be borne in mind such that the One-in-One as transcendental is not confused with a transcendence. That is, the One-in-One is not an other worldly being or even distinct from one's self. Indeed, as the last chapter made clear, the radical immanence of the One-in-One names the radical immanence of each person reading these words as distinct from their projection in the world as a subject, but also as distinct from reflection upon themselves as an I. It names in a very styptic way an unrepresentable thought. Styptic because it stops philosophy's hemorrhaging of circular self-reflection, since it posits an identity but simply as an instance of the Real that is foreclosed to representation, thought, and other forms of philosophical englobing. So the One-in-One is in this way named as transcendental as well as radically immanent (to) itself. It is transcendental to any attempt at thought, but only by virtue of its radical immanence. Going back as far as his 1981 book *Le Principe de minorité*, Laruelle has consistently implied a connection between the transcendental and radical immanence. He even writes in the 1992 book *Théorie des identités*, which preceded *Principles of Non-Philosophy*, that the transcendental is another way to say "rigorously immanent."[40] In his most recent work, as we've mentioned before, he has begun to describe this as the "immanental" in part to avoid this confusion.[41] What is important for the schematism laid out in *Principles of Non-Philosophy* is that the One-in-One axiomatically determines what precedes any Philosophical Decision. It is not a representation, since the One-in-One is never described or experienced in the philosophical sense, but is instead an axiom that structures the practice of non-philosophy. The nature of an axiom is that it functions and its veracity is accepted until it no longer functions. In so far as non-philosophy assumes a kind of indifference of the Real to philosophy's functioning – and its own – the Real or One (as One-in-One) remains as an immanental condition for thinking that itself remains radically unconditioned or prior to thought and being. How then does thought manifest itself in relation to this One-in-One?

NON(-ONE)

In his *Wissenschaftslehre* Fichte moves from the absolute unconditioned nature of the I = I (as an instance of the more common logical proposition that A = A) to something conditioned by that unconditioned: that there is a non-I or not-A (written as ~A in simple logical notation). In so far as the not-I is something it is through its relation to the I that it negates.[42] This is the way knowledge is produced in Fichte's transcendental idealism, by way of negation grounded upon a positively unconditioned identity given by an intellectual intuition. Fichte's proof of his second principle is remarkable in the way it prefigures much of phenomenological analysis and methodology, asking his readers to bring to presence their I and self-reflect upon their cognition or perception of something other than the I. Ultimately, Fichte aims to show that the conditional knowledge of objects is rooted first in the negation of the absolutely unconditioned subject. For Fichte, the not-I is the a priori sense of an object opposed to the self that is given already in the intellectual intuition of I = I:

> If I am to present anything at all, I must oppose it to the presenting self. Now within the object of presentation there can and must be an X of some sort, whereby it discloses itself as something to be presented, and not as that

which presents. But *that* everything, wherein this X may be, is not that which presents, but an item to be presented, is something that no object can teach me; for merely in order to set up something as an *object*, I have to know this already; hence it must lie initially in myself, the presenter, in advance of any possible experience.[43]

In the same way that for Fichte knowledge is produced at the most general level through the principle of opposition, in non-philosophy the explanation of philosophy's production is explained by recourse to the manifestation of a non(-One) produced through resistance to the One. Readers should note that though certain qualities of judgment are implied in terms like "opposition" and "resistance," for Fichte the term opposition is merely logical and refers to something quite literally opposite or other than the I. For Laruelle resistance is simply a description of philosophy's fundamental act. At this point the reader may be able to understand better Laruelle's claim that "Non-Philosophy is not then a logic, either dialectical or transcendental, of acts of philosophizing or indeed a logical elucidation of its statements, but rather a theory and a usage through the force-(of)-thought – so in-Real rather than logical – of the Philosophical Decision as undivided totality of its operations or acts, forms, ends and matters."[44] When he traces out the structure of the One-in-One as foreclosed to philosophy (the thinking of thought and being) his recognition of a non(-One) is then not a logical consequence, as in large part it is in Fichte, but a pragmatic analysis of philosophy itself. He writes:

> Non-philosophy, precisely in reducing the Real to its solitude of One-in-One, without logical determination or even an interiorized transcendental, opens up the possibility of the manifestation of a non(-One), of an empirical *there is* which is now that of philosophy itself, of the World, Being, Logic, etc. In effect, *if the One is absolutely indifferent, it no longer negates and can leave thought (as organon rather than ready-made or fetishized thought) to validate this resistance within certain limits or give it its "true" object.*[45]

Non-Philosophy's schematism of the One thus both accounts pragmatically for the existence of the Real as foreclosed to philosophy, but also accounts for philosophy's positive existence, its relative autonomy.

Philosophy in a certain sense is always a form of self-posited transcendence. For philosophy presents thought as limited by something other or transcendent to thought. At the same time, philosophy presents itself as the voice of that limiting transcendence, whether that be World, Being, or even Logic. For Laruelle this is ultimately a hallucination, a projection from philosophy that casts itself as its own other. For whether philosophy seeks to interpret or change the World, it still casts itself as able to co-constitute or effect the World. Philosophy's narcissism needs this, for it finds itself caught gazing at the World when the reality is that the World is just a reflection of the philosophy that gazes at it. For philosophy to avoid facing its narcissism it needs to be able to convince itself that it is not simply shadow boxing or making faces at itself in the mirror and it does so through the structure of deferral and dyads of difference traced in the theory of Philosophical Decision.

But each manifestation of Philosophical Decision arises through resistance to the unrepresentable and foreclosed essence of the One-in-One. Philosophy thus has at the core of its practice a primary negation that drives even the projects it sees as positive or as projects of affirmation. That resistance to the One-in-One does not have to manifest itself dramatically, it does not even have to register or self-present as resistance to the specific form of philosophy that is resisting. Resistance simply is the attempt to determine, co-determine, grasp, or recast the Real in some transcendent or transcendental name like World, Being, or Logic (to stick with Laruelle's examples). Importantly, however, non-philosophy does not aim to be the negation of this negation. In axiomatically casting the One as One-in-One and so foreclosed and indifferent to philosophy's resistance, it allows for the non(-One) to simply be recognized and to retain its own relative validity as a force and material.

If the One-in-One is the transcendental or, more precisely, "immanental" name of the One in its radical immanence (to) itself, then the non(-One) is the formal name for the forms of transcendence found in philosophy. The grapheme at work in Laruelle's formal writing expresses its shape. For the act of negation is at play, it is the primary or first act of philosophy in relation to the One-in-One. Yet, the best it can hope to do is suspend the One, place it between parentheses and remove it from its vision. It still remains linked to the indifferent One thereby rendering its transcendence merely relative and local. It is valid, but not absolute, owing to the radical immanence of the One.

(NON-)ONE

At this stage in the schematism Laruelle moves from axioms to a theorem and thereby departs from following closely Fichte's transcendental idealism as a model, since his contains three principles of a similar axiomatic kind. Laruelle's movement from axioms to a theorem is a recognition that, while the axioms form the basis for the practice of non-philosophy, there remains a question about how the One-in-One may determine or act upon philosophy – which claims to negate the One as the non(-One) – without bringing the One into the process of the non(-One) in a relational way:

This resistance is sufficient such that the One necessarily determines it in turn but not directly, consequently partially inside of itself, but without being obligated to renounce its real difference and to enter into a process of nega- tion, nihilation, etc., where it would alienate itself. It must be the case then, probably, in order to resolve this problem, that an organon is added to it, a thought-organon drawn from determination of resistance or of the non(-One): not directly by the One itself but, as we have said, by the One-in-the-last- instance or by this organon. The theorem of the force-(of)-thought will resolve this problem.[46]

At this stage of the guide we are now aiming to give more shape to a term that is mentioned and implied but not discussed in great depth by Laruelle: the (non-)One, which will lead us straight from the force- (of)-thought to cloning. While the theorem presented does not explicitly mention the (non-)One, we will see how it can be placed within a complete schematism of the One.

Fichte's third principle may be read as providing the form of inter- subjectivity, wherein individual subjectivity is released from a solipsistic paranoia of being the only subject in a universe of automatons and found to share and be formed in certain commonalities and shared qualities. This intersubjectivity has the added benefit of providing for the objectivity of outside experience, since it is not simply a projection of an individual subject. Of course, philosophical problems remain in the thinking of inter- subjectivity (i.e. questions of group hallucinations in psychology challenge the notion that this grounds objectivity) and this truncated summary will not answer any of them. The important point to see here is how Fichte's third principle provides a formal sketch of how intersubjectivity may be accounted for in his transcendental idealism. To explain this let us take a closer look at the principle as presented in *Principles of Non-Philosophy* and link it to the formalism found in Fichte's original text.[47]

First, take the fragment picked from that text: "I oppose in the I..." Here Fichte is proceeding with the third principle by virtue of the strengths and claims of the first two principles. We have here the principle of unconditioned identity (I = I) and the principle of opposition (there is a not-I opposed to the I). With the next part of the clause, "to the divisible I," we begin to see that the absolute identity of the I, when considered outside of its role as the unconditioned, is divisible. Fichte claims that this is by virtue of the principle of opposition. To explain this he moves from discussing it at the level of the I and the self to a more general logical notation. This will be in part why Laruelle sees in Fichte's intellectual intuition a philosophical decision that subordinates what is claimed to be unconditioned to a transcendent term like the logos. But, returning to and staying with Fichte's presentation, he says that every ~A is posited counter or opposite to A, and so A is annulled. Yet, because whatever is not A may be presented logically as simply ~A, thereby including A as part of its identity, A is not completely annulled but only annulled in part. But this means that identity is divisible between itself and not-itself. This is explained in part by linking "to the divisible I" with the rest of the sentence "a divisible non-I." While we see here the principle of opposition, we also see that there is something shared by both the I and the non-I: divisibility. Fichte explains this shared identity as follows: "Hence [A] is annulled only in part; and in place of the X in A, which is not annulled, we posit in ~A, not ~X, but X itself: and thus A = ~A in respect of X."[48] This moves us closer to understanding how the identity of the I (as I = I) may be absolute without falling into solipsism.[49] Fichte's description of this is relatively clear and is worth quoting at some length:

> Everything equated (= A = B) is equal to itself, in virtue of its being posited in the self. A = A. B = B. Now B is posited equal to A, and thus B is not posited through A; for if it was posited thereby, it would = A and not = B. (There would not be two posits, but only one). But if B is not posited through the positing of A, it to that extent = ~A; and by the equation of the two we posit neither A nor B, but an X of some sort, which = X, = A, and = B. [...] From this it is evident how the proposition A = B can be valid, though as such it contradicts the proposition A = A. X = X, A = X, B = X. Hence A = B to the extent that each = X: but A = ~B to the extent that each = ~X.[50]

This means that two different identities may be equated or shown to be grounded solely in themselves (A = A and B = B) while also being able to be posited in relation to one another without thereby grounding or conditioning their identity in the other.

It is here that we may turn back to Laruelle's mutation of Fichte's third principle and explicate it. Owing to its complexity let us quote it again before moving on. "The One-in-One is the identity-in-the-last-instance of the unilateral duality of the indivisible One and the divisible *and* indivisible non(-One); this identity is the organon of thought or force-(of)-thought, as solution to the problem of the determination of the non(-One) by the One."[51] In simpler terms, since the One-in-One cannot be represented and is indifferent to the non(-One), how can we account for how it determines the non(-One) without falling back into certain metaphysical formulations that move non-philosophy towards standard Philosophical Decision? Harkening back to our discussion of Gödel numbering in Chapter 2, we may say that Laruelle's solution to this problem is to find a way to manifest a more complex thought in simpler notation. That is, the One-in-One remains indifferent to the non(-One), so is not rooted or determined or even co-determined by it and this non-relation is structured according to unilateral duality such that in-the-last-instance the non(-One) only exists from its own relative perspective, while from the One-in-One there is only its radical (and not absolute) identity as radical immanence. This presents an analogous problem to Fichte's outlined earlier: how can this non-relation or unilateral determination be thought if the One-in-One is foreclosed to thought and representation? By virtue of thinking the identity together simply as (non-)One. That is, there is an identity of the unilateral duality of the One-in-One (radical immanence) and the non(-One) (philosophical transcendence) that is manifest as (non-)One (transcendental or philosophical quasi-immanence).[52] In other words, the (non-)One suspends philosophy's relative negation in order to posit a positive effect of the One, but only as a clone since the One-in-One is indifferent. But this of course begs the question, what does Laruelle mean by a clone?

RESISTANCE AND CLONING

In this concluding section to the chapter, we will highlight first a philosophical operation and its parallel in non-philosophy: philosophical resistance and cloning, which can be mapped onto our schematism as non(-One) and (non-)One. Laruelle writes:

> As reaction to the foreclosure of the One, but which the One opposes to thought, there is resistance that is philosophical in origin (in the sense whereby philosophy is its place and its body) and which manifests itself empirically first of all. Resistance or the non(-One) is by definition a "more" real thing than logical opposition, which is not real, and even more purely real "in-the-last-instance" than the semi-real semi-logical opposition of the I and the non-I.[53]

While readers should note that Laruelle here marks out the distinction between himself and Fichte again (Fichte's foundational principles being logical in nature and Laruelle's being "real" or according to the causal structure of the Real as DLI), the implication here is that resistance is how philosophy produces itself. In a limited but nonetheless important sense resistance then is the production of thought.

This philosophical act can only be called resistance, because it is always only a relative negation. Philosophy's attempt to negate the indifference of the Real by attempting to englobe or encompass it within transcendent names like Being or Other or Truth, etc., never actually absolutely negates the Real or the One. It is thus only constituted as resistance to the foreclosed Real's unrepresentablity. This sense of resistance as productive of thought may help to explain a statement in *Philosophies of Difference* which struck Graham Harman as especially egregious, writing of it that, "If there is a

80

more bizarre passage in recent philosophy, or a more twisted sentiment, it is unknown to me."[54]

The statement he glosses is worth quoting at length, both because it is a moment of rhetorical power in Laruelle that contains a clarity he is often accused of lacking, and because Harman's gloss serves to obscure the real core of the claim:

> Thus all contemporary philosophy of Difference [referring to Nietzsche, Heidegger, Derrida, and Deleuze] offers despite everything a strangely Platonizing spectacle: the interminable procession of the most communal entities, Being, Nothingness, Desire, Power, Language, Text, raising themselves up from the ground of experience each in turn like shades at once bloodless and laden with chains, trying to lift themselves in infinite file towards a mirage of the One where they would believe themselves capable being regenerated and saved from empirical hell as at a wellspring of life. It is truly a bizarre and certainly "philosophical" merry-go-round, philosophical because it is simultaneously ascending and descending and playing itself out finally in a circle and in place. As if these larvae wished, by their hesitations, their stumblings, their skiddings, the allure of their approach continually spoiled, to abandon the weighty forms of being or non-being in order to yield and sink into their limit, to abandon their determined forms of existence, to prove to themselves that they still exist when in truth they exist only as fleeting larvae on the earth. They seek the One precisely because they have not found it, and they will never find anything other than what they already are: them-'selves'. They possess no more than tautological life, but they still do not know that tautological existence does not exhaust the real, that Being, Nothingness, Desire, Text, Power, etc., all this is absurd and these tautologies are unnecessary. They have their aims, hatreds and desires, but they continue to be unaware that if they possess sense as relative to one another and truth as relative to them*selves* and as a system of them all, all this taken together – and *taken together*, the system itself included as well, which cannot exceed or escape itself and its destiny – is as absurd and unnecessary as a tautology. For the One, the World is a redundancy.[55]

While Harman sees this as evidence of Laruelle taking on the persona of Grand Moff Tarkin, referring to the Star Wars villain who destroys a planet, the power of this rhetoric speaks more of a kind of St. Francis or Girolamo Savonarola preaching against the World and the ways in which people confuse worldly wealth and prestige with a truthful or real recognition. Or, if the religious link to "zealots" like Francis and Savonarola is too much for some readers, imagine Laruelle here in the role of the best friend in a romantic comedy telling the star (the philosopher, for philosophers are always the stars of their own movies) that he is simply trying too hard to impress his love (the World) and furthermore that this love interest is not the person the philosopher believes her to be (a hallucination). "She's just not that into you," he remarks to the overwrought attempts of the philosopher continually peacocking and pestering the love interest.

This example, perhaps as ludicrous as Harman's mocking reference to Star Wars, does allow us an example of how resistance produces creativity. For just as the spurned lover creates elaborate plans and productions to impress the lover, so do concepts and ideas emerge from the philosopher in his or her resistance to the One or the Real. Laruelle's tone in *Philosophies of Difference* is more indignant than in *Principles of Non-Philosophy*, but this is true generally of the period of Philosophy II, which sought to subordinate philosophy to science, whereas in Philosophy III (where, again, *Principles of Non-Philosophy* is located) the goal is to create a unified theory, to further remove thinking from the philosophical game of sufficiency. For, remember, this schematism of the One and the description of philosophy's resistance is part and parcel of an investigation of philosophy as the source of the World's projection, so this schema does not represent the unrepresentable or eff the ineffable Real in philosophical terms. In some sense there is a submission to the Real, which Laruelle has recently referred to as "underdetermination," but this submission is not couched in hierarchical terms, rather it should be understood in the same sense as when one "goes under" anesthesia. We also see, then, that the goal is not something like a worship or dogmatic theology of the One. Laruelle aims to do something with the force-(of)-thought clearly manifest in philosophy and to do that he has to first provide an accurate model of what the force-(of)-thought is. It is not simply philosophical resistance, but resistance as still One in-the-last-instance, which schematically takes on the notation of (non-)One as a kind of suspension of philosophy's negativity but also signifying that this One is not the One-in-One, but it is still preceded by it.

Since the One-in-One is pure immanence it cannot "act" in a philosophically meaningful way, leading to the question of how the One is able to present or manifest itself, a question we have already touched upon in the schematism. We saw there that the response to that problem is found in the description of the force-(of)-thought and written in the schematism as (non-)One. Laruelle also gives this another name, and one that moves away from the purely schematic to something like a Deleuzian conceptual persona: the clone. He explicitly links the clone to this solution, writing: "There will be a definitive solution to this problem and it will have the same degree of 'truth' or immanence as the axiom of the One-in-One itself, precisely because being 'in-the-last-instance,' this immanence only transmits itself and itself alone – this is cloning."[56] The force-(of)-thought then is a clone as the same solution to the problem, as he explicitly states in the *Dictionary of Non-Philosophy* under the definition for force-(of)-thought.[57]

Casting the force-(of)-thought as a clone at least in part explains how the One-in-One may act without being lost in the material or being co-constituted by it. While Laruelle has elsewhere differentiated his sense of cloning from the "biotechnological" act of cloning, we may begin to understand what attracts him to this persona by noticing again that the clone is not a mere copy of an original.[58] Neither is it a reflection upon something other than it. The clone retains its own identity, thereby not being a reflection or copy, but carries the same genetic structure as the material it is cloned from. In this way the clone carries forth the essence of the One in its action, without this action being able to be claimed in any meaningful sense of the One. Furthermore, the One is not confused with the material that the clone acts upon and does not risk the alienation of its identity.

While reference to speculation has recently become popular again, Laruelle locates the drive to speculation as the philosophical act *par excellence*. The notion of speculation is related to the mirror and comes to us in English and French from the verb *specere* which is in turn related to the noun *speculum*, the Latin for "mirror" as well as "copy." In many ways the structure of Philosophical Decision is very clearly the structure of a mirror, and so since force-(of)-thought is the non-philosophical cloning of various forms of Philosophical Decision, recasting them in-One, it is unsurprising to find that it carries forward the speculative spirit for non-philosophy. Laruelle is clear that he is not interested in breaking the mirror of speculation, that philosophy's act of speculating is not on trial, though it should be noted that when he speaks pejoratively of it he tends to use the term "specular," referring in part to philosophy's narcissism. In this vein he writes, "The belief in the absolute elimination of the specular is a philosophical one, as we have said, and leads to a failure and a simple repression. What is possible and positive is the *radical* (and not "absolute") invalidation of the structure of the mix or the double which affects the mirror/reflection duality, and the manifestation of its transcendental identity."[59] In other words, rather than aiming to end speculation, non-philosophy simply breaks speculation's *mise-en-abyme* and does so through DLI and the recognition of speculation's transcendental or "rigorously immanent" identity in-the-last-instance as in-One. The clone, however, allows us to still speak, to still create, to still fashion something from the material of philosophy, without falling into the hallucination that is philosophy's casting of the World we are supposedly thrown into. As Laruelle states in *Intellectuals and Power: The Insurrection of the Victim*, linking this cold abstraction to the realm of ethics:

> what I call cloning is not biological – which is to say inhuman – but is more the essence of human action. [...] The clone that I speak about is not an

extra-terrestrial, it is extraworldly. Even "extraworldly" is not the best formula because it lets one assume that first there is the World and then comes Man. From the outset Man puts the World to the test before the World tests Man – the World as already given in the human mode. This is what causes the human subject, Man as Stranger-subject, to be thrown necessarily into the World, more so than Heidegger ever imagined. The Name-of-Man symbolizes this righteousness which will go from utopia to the World.[60]

And so we end this chapter returning to the impetus of non-philosophy's abstraction: to be a pragmatic theory of philosophy in terms of the human as last-instance.

5

Dualysis: Or, How To Do Things With Philosophy

As *Principles of Non-Philosophy* develops, cloning is one of the hinge points that connects Chapter 4 to Chapter 5, "The Method of Dualysis: (Performance, Cloning, A Priori)." As we move from the discussion of non-philosophical causality to the method of dualysis it would not be accurate to say that they are distinct, since cloning is both part of the causality modeled in the previous chapter and the method to be situated in this one. Cloning is an aspect of the method within the wider method of non-philosophy's dualysis of philosophy, a dualysis that Laruelle says non-philosophy uses to think and act upon philosophical material without making the corollary claim that the Real is acted upon or circumscribed within thought. Dualysis is a way of beginning to do things with the Philosophical Decision. Since Philosophical Decision is a structure that generates dualisms, non-philosophy takes this dualism as an object. Note that what is taken is the two terms *and* their relation to one another, all three terms together as a single object, the entire 2/3 or 3/2 structure of philosophy traced out in previous chapters. In doing this, non-philosophy avoids the philosophical operation of division, and cloning here is key: "*Dualysis does not divide its object; it proceeds by cloning it in the mode of unilateral duality.*"[1] It is precisely in taking the three objects and cloning them as a single projection in the mode of unilateral duality that Laruelle may begin to do creative things with the material of philosophy, with what is produced in particular instances but invariantly under the structure of Philosophical Decision.

But if this is to be truly non-philosophical it must operate differently than philosophy when it claims to transcend other regional knowledges, to speak for what they doing. Laruelle tells us that when philosophy enters into relation with these regional forms of knowing, it casts itself as the driving force at work: "Philosophy is thus the 'superior form' of a regional knowing that it takes from elsewhere, and which remains partly contingent."[2] He goes on delineate the various names given to these proclaimed "superior forms":

> It can be called, in terms of these already constituted objects of knowing, "transcendental geometry", "transcendental topology", "transcendental linguistics", "transcendental aesthetics", "transcendental sophistry", etc: it is susceptible to multiple possibilities where the transcendental is always blended with the empirical and never attains the "purity" to which it is susceptible when it results from the Real-One.[3]

Non-Philosophy will be different in so far as it will be an immanental entering into these very blended forms of thinking (though he retains the use of the term transcendental in *Principles of Non-Philosophy*) and thinking them precisely under the condition of the Real-One. While we may be thankful that Laruelle has written "purity" with the requisite scare quotes, what we will have is a form of thinking where in-the-last-instance there is no distinction between the transcendental and the empirical. There will be no blend of thought, because there will be separation, and instead we will have material to build with.

Non-Philosophy aims to be a "solution producing knowledges" rather than a philosophical challenge or "a new philosophical decision."[4] That requires then that as a method non-philosophy be a way of doing something with the material philosophical debates produce. Dualysis is the method that allows for that. So, in this chapter, our main aim is to bring out the nature of dualysis generally by tracing three specific instances of it that can be located in Chapter 5 of *Principles of Non-Philosophy*. Each dualysis is tied to a specific amphibology or intertwined dualism as produced by Philosophical Decision. The first amphibology is the Jewgreek or Greekjew nature of European philosophy. This diagnosis of philosophy, first made by Derrida, allows us to examine the vacillation in twentieth-century European philosophy between Being and Alterity or Otherness as the basis of its practice. The second amphibology is between myth and reason. Here we locate Laruelle's fittingness with critical theory as represented by Horkheimer and Adorno and then sketch possible future lines of research that take up certain tools from non-philosophy for questions that critical theory has illuminated. Finally, we look at the amphibology of life and death in the works of Henry and Brassier. In the first amphibology we also explore the concept of performation, while in the third we explore the meaning of a priori for Laruelle (leaving our exploration of cloning in the previous chapter to do the work of helping the reader make sense of the concept in this one).

In each case we will find that Laruelle turns to radical forms of philosophy. Radical philosophies are the locus of his critique since they are the ones that offer the most suitable materials to build with and to which non-philosophy has a family resemblance because of its use of them. These radical philosophies, whether deconstruction or philosophies of immanence or some other form, are often taken to be challenges to the philosophical establishment. In distinction, non-philosophy aims to do something with philosophy as such.

"JEWGREEK IS GREEKJEW": THE DUALYSIS OF CONTEMPORARY PHILOSOPHY'S AMPHIBOLOGY OF BEING AND ALTERITY

As noted, Laruelle discusses various forms of philosophy that have been said to have a family resemblance to non-philosophy. He focuses on one of these as particularly important, in terms both of its influence upon non-philosophy and of the need to differentiate the two projects. He calls this the "Judaic turn of philosophy," a term that he uses both in *Principles of Non-Philosophy* and *Philosophies of Difference*. The second of these books was the focus of a critical review essay by Andrew McGettigan in the journal *Radical Philosophy*.[5] Laruelle's differentiation of non-philosophy from this Judaic turn is interesting in its own right and is clearly an important influence. The "turn" encompasses a move in philosophy that he considers radical in many respects and has promoted throughout his career.[6] However, I am directing your attention to this term precisely because it has been the occasion for some critics to display their misunderstanding of Laruelle's understanding of the history of philosophy and, at times, has been misconstrued as an example of Laruelle's egregious "essentialism" that belies a kind of intellectual anti-Semitism. I consider this a serious charge that requires a response on that basis alone. However, it also concerns a fundamental misunderstanding of the practical goal of non-philosophy, which is to defend human beings from certain overbearing determinations that harass the human and claim to capture its clandestine identity in easier markers of identity. While, as we will see, Laruelle is critical of philosophical universalism, he does aim for a kind of generic vision of the human as a model of the human's radical immanence. Thus, while certain nuances regarding the particularities of identity (race, gender, culture, religion, etc.) still need to be worked out non-philosophically, Laruelle's project is thoroughly rooted in an anti-racist core.[7] Such anti-racism may easily be missed, especially in highly programmatic and abstract texts like *Principles of Non-Philosophy* or *Philosophies of Difference*; it appears to be an explicitly hoped for by-product of that abstract disempowering of philosophy's harassing force. As he remarks in a conversation with Robin Mackay:

> If, within non-standard thought [another name for non-philosophy], the knowledge of human nature (to put it in traditional terms) remains entirely problematic, not at all becoming the object of some dogmatic knowledge, this only goes to show that there is no absolutely determined knowledge of the human, of man; and in particular it aids the struggle against every dogmatic definition of human nature – against racism, for example: if one has no absolutely certain knowledge of human nature, it is far more difficult to develop a racist thought.[8]

And so not only can we attempt to rectify the poor reading of Laruelle offered by an outraged and confused critic, we may also see dualysis at work in the way the Jew/Greek amphibology of philosophy is located and recast as material instances by Laruelle.

Let us begin with McGettigan's confusion of certain descriptions of the philosophical work of Derrida and Levinas with anti-Semitic "epithets," when they are actually descriptions of their work *qua* philosophy. He lists three: *duplice, retors,* and *furtif*.[9] If these were anti-Semitic tropes endemic to Laruelle's philosophy we might have expected Derrida himself to have raised them in his responses to Laruelle's *Philosophies of Difference* as well as to have seen these tropes repeated throughout Laruelle's own discussion of the Judaic turn in philosophy. But, while the decisions on how to translate these terms are ultimately part of McGettigan's attempt to cast aspersions upon Laruelle, they do not appear in *Principles of Non-Philosophy* with reference to Derrida or Levinas. Nor do they appear in reference to psychoanalysis; though McGettigan does not appear to know that Laruelle considers this discipline to be a part of the Judaic turn, despite being practiced by subjects who take on designations other than Jewish (like the Catholic Lacan). The reason for this adjective being used to describe a *turn* and not subjects will become clearer in a moment. But all three terms mirror Laruelle's critique, not of religion or a religious community and tradition, but of *philosophy*. Duplicity relates to the split nature of philosophy as such, into Greek and Jewish modalities, casting itself at times as empirical and at other times as transcendental, owing to its fundamental amphibology, and discussed explicitly by Laruelle in relation to the double-band illuminated by Derrida.[10] *Retors*, which McGettigan translates as crafty, may also be translated as "twisty" or "wily," referring again to philosophy's fundamentally ambiguous nature used always to its own advantage and the way it forms a twisted loop with itself. These are not epithets in any meaningful sense, but McGettigan discloses a fundamental confusion when he presents them as being directed towards Derrida and Levinas as Jews when he writes, "That such epithets appear in a context depicting Derrida and Levinas as Jews is crass."[11] However, despite McGettigan's protestations that they are philosophers, Levinas and Derrida also draw explicitly and unashamedly on their being situated within the Jewish tradition. There is no fundamental incompatibility between being a philosopher and a Jew or taking concepts or ideas from the Jewish tradition and casting them philosophically, even if the goal is to undermine certain authoritarian aspects of philosophy as it was for Levinas. Before turning to the way that dualysis is practiced by Laruelle, the reader should first understand that especially as regards the question of European philosophy's identity post-World War II, Laruelle looks to the model provided by Derrida himself and which Derrida eventually takes on in a very personal way as he writes of the struggles he has to think through his own identity.[12] Contra McGettigan's claims, Laruelle is not acting out some anti-Semitic logic in locating an amphibology in European philosophy of (Greek) Being and (Jewish) Alterity. Indeed, he is following Derrida himself, who does not deny the fundamentally Jewgreek nature of philosophy nor decry Jews as somehow outside of philosophy in some simplistic sense, but points towards the fundamentally Jewgreek nature of the phenomenological tradition he deconstructed. The Greek and the Jew are identities that circulate in various ways and thus should be analyzed for how they circulate *qua* philosophy.

Let us leave aside now these charges bordering on slander and use the occasion as an opportunity to deal with the more interesting issue being investigated by Laruelle: the shape of contemporary philosophy after the triple challenges of psychoanalysis, ethics as first philosophy, and deconstruction. For Laruelle the heart of European philosophy is Jewgreek/Greekjew. He writes:

> All of the "continental" history of thought after Nietzsche and with Freud, Wittgenstein, Lacan, Derrida, etc., can be condensed into the history of a fight between Being and the Other (more simply: these terms suffice to show what is involved here), a fight between Greek ontology and Judaism through psychoanalysis and "deconstructions" which will have given a new seat to the old conflict of philosophy and the Human Sciences.[13]

This sense of contemporary European philosophy having a fundamentally mixed identity comes from Laruelle's study of Derrida. At the end of "Violence and Metaphysics" Derrida famously quotes James Joyce's "Jewgreek is greekjew. Extremes meet," but places it within a litany of questions, beginning with "Are we Greeks? Are we Jews? But who, we? Are we (not a chronological, but a pre-logical question) *first* Jews or *first* Greeks?"[14] The very possibility of asking this question is Levinas' challenge to Heideggerian ontology which claims that "The entirety of philosophy is conceived on the basis of its Greek source."[15] Levinas' challenge comes through a return to ethics as facilitated by the irreducible experience of the Other which is "experience par excellence."[16] Ethics takes thinking to a place or "non-place" beyond Being, to pure experience, to the things themselves shorn of their theoretical overdeterminations. This non-place happens in the face-to-face encounter, a repetition of an experience of transcendence beyond ontology's theoretical grasp that Levinas calls religion, and a relation he claims is a religious relation.[17]

This appeal to transcendence in Levinas is part and parcel of his attempt to overturn the totalitarianism within Greek philosophy. It is the rupturing of a vision of the world as a totality, where being determines ethics or where ethics is subordinated to the logic of being (ontology) and thus to the logic of sameness. It is in Derrida's deconstruction of Levinas that we can start to see one way in which Laruelle developed the methods of non-philosophy after his apprenticeship in deconstruction. For Derrida sees Levinas' attempt to undercut philosophy's authority through an appeal to experience as a way in which philosophy is able to justify its existence once again. He writes:

> But empiricism always has been determined by philosophy, from Plato to Husserl, as *nonphilosophy*: as the philosophical pretention to nonphilosophy, the inability to justify oneself, to come to one's own aid as speech. But this incapacitation, when resolutely assumed, contests the resolution and coherence of the logos (philosophy) at its root, instead of letting itself be questioned by the logos. Therefore, nothing can so profoundly *solicit* the Greek logos – philosophy – than this irruption of the totally-other; and nothing can to such an extant reawaken the logos as to its origin as to its mortality, its other.[18]

We see here a nascent sense of the structure of Philosophical Decision, one now where the Other comes to be what solicits a kind of third term of unity. And while Derrida is deconstructing Levinas here, he is not rejecting the Other as a necessary philosophical trope in so far as it *solicits* the logos or even a thinking of Being. It is on this basis that Laruelle can claim, "Whatever there may be in each of these avatars that no longer interest us in their diversity, thought is definitively installed in the milieu of this Judaic turn; a new economy of relations of the Philosophical Decision and the Other is fixed bit by bit in order to form *the new common sense of philosophers*."[19]

What is this common sense? Well, let us look once more at Derrida and consider his statement, "Are we Jews? Are we Greeks? We live in the difference between the Jew and the Greek, which is perhaps the unity of what is called history. We live in and of difference, that is, in *hypocrisy*."[20] The common sense is not one of conversion to Judaism. But a certain kind of identity is produced through the difference of Greek and Jewish sources of thought. With the rise of psychoanalysis, ethics as first philosophy, and deconstruction, the Other comes to be a philosophical assumption, something one has to engage with in any philosophical project. Now, contra McGettigan, Laruelle is not making a claim here that the identity of philosophy is threatened by Judaism or Jewish thought. Indeed, this adjective refers simply to the focus on the Other, and in *Principles of Non-Philosophy* and elsewhere he differentiates various particular forms of this general Judaic turn along the three lines we have mentioned already. In Laruelle's view this is a positive move, an important movement within philosophy, and he claims in an interview that "Judaism has become the principle interlocutor of philosophy. [...] Under these different forms, Judaism has become a criterion for the humanity and internal ethical capacity of philosophy. And it is true that, without Judaism, philosophy would probably be boring, dogmatic, and very inhumane (apart from Deleuze, anyway...)."[21]

However, this introduction of Judaism into philosophy is still philo-sophically determined. Philosophy is changed by it, made more ethical or human, less boring, but it remains philosophy. This is Laruelle's focus and it is on this basis that the form of philosophy is criticized, not Judaism as such, but the double or joint authority of contemporary philosophy.[22] And so the Jewgreek/Greekjew mixture comes to be another philosophical duality, not a cultural identity, but a form of thinking that is constitutive of how a cultural identity is seen and interpreted. That is, a philosophy that lends itself to being dualyzed. Let's look at where Laruelle summarizes non-philosophy's absolute commencement with the radical immanence of the human prior to any determination of "human nature" and the way this allows him to think and recast the Greco-Judaic duality of contemporary philosophy.

> The "historical" signification of non-philosophy is established thus: it is neither Greek nor Judaic, nor the crossbreeding of the two, but *the ante-Greek and ante-Judaic identity of thought, the experience of thought "before" its Greco-Judaic disjunction*. It substitutes for the terrain of Being, that of ontological difference – the philosophical tradition up to and including Nietzsche – and for the terrain of the Other – that of the Greco-Judaic interferences of the twentieth century since Freud and Wittgenstein – the new terrain of the One not "*qua* one" but as it is or One-in-One.[23]

In the duality of Being and the Other, we now have disempowered those terms as transcendental fields or terrains and instead cast them as materials that are found only on the terrain of the One-in-One. In-One there is no Jew or Greek. Importantly, and marking a difference from the Pauline Christian conversion of Jew and Greek into "a new race," the Jew or Greek is not converted into One, because the One is indifferent to such conversion and in-the-last-instance the Jew or Greek already is in-One.

We can see this point made abstractly by Laruelle when he explains the different aspects or sides of philosophy acted upon through cloning and dualysis:

> Consequently, non-philosophy is very exactly, through the force-(of)-thought, a *transcendental cloning and a dualysis* of the philosophical materials. This method, grasped from the side of duality, can be said in effect to be a dualysis as it is said to be a cloning when it is seized from the side of identity. Being only transcendental and not equally real, non-philosophy cannot broach the mixed-form but suspends its validity and thus distinguishes, as we have said, the a priori residue of the mix and the mix itself as support having abandoned its auto-positional claim.[24]

We see here that dualysis is said to affect the side of philosophy's duality, while cloning affects the side of its identity. Hence in the method of non-philosophy we can see what Laruelle has done with the philosophical materials – dualysis flowing from the philosophies of Alterity and cloning from those of Being. As he goes on to say, the mixed nature of European philosophy is not treated as real, but is instead subject to being acted upon in order to distinguish and recast its aspects and what Laruelle refers to as its a priori residue. From the already-manifest and unrepresentable perspective of the Real, neither Greekness nor Jewishness is real, but that does not mean that they are not active, or that they do not exist (since existence is a predicate that cannot be applied to the Real), or are not constitutive of a reality that should not be confused with the Real itself. It is a matter of recognizing how they exist in the World projected by philosophy (and its attendant forms of thought such as politics) without such recognition itself being cast as valid or totalizing.

Such "non-recognition" is one way to understand what Laruelle calls performation. He summarizes performation by contrasting it with the more familiar concept of performativity:

> We call performation – rather than performativity, which indicates a general property – the operation of the force-(of)-thought, its activity of immanent organon. [...] The force-(of)-thought is such that the intention, end or effect of the act are immediately realized with the act itself, without any division

or transcendent distinction being able to slide between them and differentiate what emerges in one piece. [...] Performational immanence can only be in-the-last-instance, which is to say never given in the already constituted milieu of transcendence, even if this immanence is the essence of a simple or non-autopositional transcending.[25]

Much about this claim should now be foregrounded for the reader, in particular the emphasis on immanence, an operation where thought takes place without any sense of division, where in some sense nothing happens at all since this performation takes place outside the frame of representational philosophy. But in the dualysis of the Jewgreek nature of philosophy undertaken in *Philosophies of Difference* we find an example of this performation as witnessed in the very way *Principles of Non-Philosophy* acts out a thought of cloning and dualysis in its dualysis of Being and Other, Identity and Duality. While it is referred to in later texts by Laruelle, performation does not figure as a major concept going forward for non-philosophy. Its importance lies in how it helps us to understand the character and aims of non-philosophical dualysis. I have characterized it as a form of "non-recognition" because it shows how non-philosophy's casting of materials takes place in a distinctly relative deflationary way. Thus, the performation of European philosophy undercuts any claims to totality or even the validity of the hierarchical form of thought found there, but does so while bearing witness to the distinctive power of that thought regardless of its relative nature.

To return to McGettigan's contention that Laruelle crassly and baselessly casts Derrida and Levinas as Jewish philosophers, one might hastily come to the conclusion that the argument here seeks to reconcile Laruelle to McGettigan's valorization of the secular and universal character of philosophy. Critics of philosophies and theories imbricated with what is sometimes referred to as "identity politics" may think that in Laruelle they have found another philosopher like Badiou or Žižek, who emphasizes the need for a concept of universality where instances of gender, racial, or other identities are subtracted to get to the real human core. But the reality is far more nuanced and fecund. For, unlike European philosophy's claim to universalism, Laruelle's performation of European philosophy requires that the particularity underlying philosophy's claim to universality be faced, disempowered, and cast as material as well. While he is of course not the first thinker to make this claim, non-philosophy's rigor does offer another resource and tool for doing something with philosophy, another way of melting down the master's tools so that something truly human may be built.[26]

THE COUNTERFEIT UNIVERSAL: THE AMBHIBOLOGY OF REASON AND MYTHOLOGY

This Jewgreek/Greekjew identity of philosophy hints at another fundamental dualism at the heart of philosophy's functioning important for the critique of philosophy developed by Laruelle: the dualism of reason and myth. Philosophy has traditionally cast itself against myth. This is true of those forms of philosophy which have been denigrated in the twentieth century for their excessive focus on reason against embodiment, for example Cartesian philosophy, but it is also true of the most radical forms of philosophy like that of Deleuze who writes (with Guattari):

> Whenever there is transcendence, vertical Being, imperial State in the sky or on earth, there is religion [myth]; and there is Philosophy whenever there is immanence, even if it functions as arena for the agon and rivalry (the Greek tyrants do not constitute an objection to this, because they are wholeheartedly on the side of the society of friends such as it appears in their wildest, most violent rivalries).[27]

And yet, Laruelle's claim will be that ultimately philosophy is a form of myth that needs its own critique, its own process of demythologization. What makes philosophy in part a form of myth is its relation to the Real, "Like any mythology, philosophy believes it can decide the Real or even know it."[28]

European philosophy casts itself as true knowing but in so doing enters into the mythological field as a new driving force akin to the transcendental empiricism or transcendental geometry described in the introduction to this chapter. Here we find a new form of philosophy to add to that list: "Subject to the limits of this type of definition, limits which come from the diversity and contingency of objects of knowing with which they identify themselves, we can equally define philosophy as 'transcendental mythology,' a 'superior' form of mythological knowing – or of supposed knowing, mythology functioning *as* knowing."[29] It is important to see that Laruelle is not following the standard philosophical denigration of myth by philosophy here. His point is not that philosophy is somehow the real mythology that must fall to a weaponized form of science or what is sometimes called scientism. To understand his more subtle argument we need to step back and see how both reason and modernity are understood by Laruelle. In sum, however, the amphibology of European philosophy could be stated as reason is mythological and myth is rational. This amphibology will be utilized by Laruelle, but first let us see if we can locate it comparatively with the diagnosis of two other thinkers.

Laruelle first discusses the ways in which philosophy has battled the mythos before stating:

The old fight against mythos is complicated, nuanced, differentiated, but mythos is only even more involved and installed here at the more and more rational heart of the logos. Given this situation, if we must have a thought that we could really call "modern", we must also break with *the philosophical tradition of modernity* (Plato, Descartes, Husserl, etc.) and its rationalism, which is to say its usage of science in terms of Mythological Difference.[30]

While there is no textual evidence that Laruelle is here intentionally drawing upon Frankfurt School critique, this statement strongly resonates with the criticisms present in Max Horkheimer and Theodor Adorno's *Dialectic of Enlightenment* and reading them in conjunction may help readers to place Laruelle's own sense of myth at play. In Horkheimer and Adorno's text, written towards the end of the Nazi's reign of terror and genocide, they trace the ways in which the dream of Enlightenment self-mastery has slipped into the worst sort of barbarisms and find that "Enlightenment's mythic terror springs forth from a horror of myth."[31] As they go on to argue throughout the rest of the text, Enlightenment philosophy and culture gives birth to a will to objectivity, to the rising supremacy of reason over other forms of knowledge. In order to unpack this claim Horkheimer and Adorno undertake a reading of the myth of Odysseus as bearing "witness to the dialectic of enlightenment."[32] In this reading science is overdetermined by the dialectic of enlightenment, put to work for the rationalizing of labor – that is, the organization of labor in the right measure so that working people aren't utterly destroyed (or at least not destroyed too early) and the maximal amount of profit can be extracted from them.

Part of this rationalization of labor requires a certain mythologization of the practice of science itself, where science is able to operate in the "objective" realm as opposed to the subjective focus of myth. It is important not simply to collapse Horkheimer and Adorno's sense of myth with Laruelle's, but we can see here that they recognize something like the dyad that Laruelle argues is produced by the Philosophical Decision. And like Laruelle they locate a third term, in their case Odysseus as representative of the capitalist landowner and boss, that is able to unite the objective (realm of reason) and the subjective (realm of myth). Odysseus is able to unite these realms in a way that, though not entirely faithful to Horkheimer and Adorno's reading, may help us to understand the modernity that Laruelle contrasts to a possible "non-modernity" when he writes: "The 'non-modernity' of thought is not the modernity of philosophy which uses science in an inegalitarian manner to its own profit. It [i.e. non-modernity] delivers itself not only from constituted mythology, but also from mythological Difference itself, which is to say the authority of philosophy."[33] Odysseus and his men act as a persona of the modernity of the philosophers in the way they bring together the dyad of objective and subjective witnessed in the familiar story of the Sirens. In the original story Odysseus and his men are counseled that they will soon approach the Sirens whose seductive song invariably leads to shipwreck. In order to navigate past them Odysseus instructs his men to plug their eyes with beeswax, but he wishes to hear the song and so orders them to fasten him to the mast so that he cannot take control of the ship and give in to the seduction. Odysseus, in this instance, is made safe to flirt with the temptation to fanaticism, to flirt with the realms of madness and to glimpse something like the Real promised in the Sirens' call to know the future and thereby master the past. Yet those who must labor, who are not considered safe to glimpse the Real lest they slip into the fanaticism of myth, must be made deaf, unable to hear the truth in a form of philosophical deflation. That is, they are made to serve the modern persona par excellence, he who can glimpse the messianic, mythic promise of reason only by subjecting those placed beneath him to a process of demythologization.

Horkheimer and Adorno gave the subtitle *Philosophical Fragments* to their *Dialectic of Enlightenment* and this witnesses to the descriptive element of their theory. In this mode their critical theory was not proscriptive. Here Laruelle's own analysis of the amphibologies of Philosophical Decision may enter into fruitful dialogue with these early forms of Frankfurt critical theory. Horkheimer and Adorno end their critique of the dialectic of enlightenment with the claim that "Enlightenment itself, having mastered itself and assumed its own power, could break through the limits of enlightenment."[34] Clearly their goal was not simply a decision in favor of myth against enlightenment reason or vice versa, but the construction of something beyond this dyad. Like them, we find Laruelle not simply subjecting philosophy to the positive sciences as the true fonts of (objective) knowing, nor, as we have seen throughout this text, does he subject science to the force of myth. But, also like Horkheimer and Adorno, we do find him attempting to construct something pragmatic using the amphibological dyad as material. In a similar sense with which they recover the term enlightenment, Laruelle will recast mythology and modernity as "non-mythology" and "non-modernity," clones of their standard, philosophically overdetermined iterations whose codes may be exploited for human use when deprived of their claims to the very horizon of thought itself.

So the very process of dualysis, locating dyads produced by Philosophical Decision, is productive of doing something with philosophy as material. Importantly, one of the aspects of philosophy's practice located by Laruelle is a philosophical faith at play which, like all myth according to him, believes that it can affect and know the Real. And it does so through philosophy's decisional apparatus. One of those decisions is found in philosophy's claim to demythologize human knowledge. Yet we can begin to do things with philosophy when we begin to practice a demythologization of philosophy itself: "For the philosophical demythization or demythologization of thought we substitute the demythologization of philosophy itself, and better still: a 'non-mythology'."[35] The first move in carrying out such a demythologization is to identify philosophy's activity. One aspect of the magical thinking that arises from mythology concerns the arbitrary nature of certain signs. Thus, to take an often mocked example, when enframed by a certain mythology, a person may ascribe special significance to what is taken to be an image of Christ in a piece of burnt toast. In this case there is a lack of communal ritualization, and so the ridiculousness of the claim to significance is readily accepted by the wider community. But scholars of religion know that the arbitrariness of mythological thinking is ultimately similar to the arbitrariness of the image of Christ in the toast, only that the arbitrary nature of accepted myths is usually covered over through ritualization. And here I invite the reader of philosophy to consider the ritual nature of the practice of philosophy by philosophers at conferences, in papers, and through the construction of certain forms of reading. In many ways, scholars outside of philosophy may more readily accept certain claims that Laruelle puts forth regarding the relative nature of philosophy as a discourse. Such a view already exists, for example, in anthropology and ethnography. While Laruelle would likely want to interrogate certain philosophical survivals in these discourses, he would join with anthropologists like Talal Asad who are doing the same work. With regard to ritualization and mythology, readers may find the work of Catherine Bell of use.[36] Isomorphically to Laruelle's critique of philosophy's arbitrary nature, Bell takes great pains to show the ways in which ritual theory may enter into a vicious circle by projecting an image of ritual that is simply another iteration of ritual theory rather than an actual object. Compare then the isomorphic way that Laruelle describes philosophy as undertaking its task arbitrarily: "To philosophize is to move from a given *assumed as real* ... toward its grounding, horizon, condition, etc. We say *assumed* because it is taken at random from the experience of circumstances and especially from experience conceived as transcendent or inscribed in the form of auto-position."[37] This arbitrary nature may go some way towards an alternative explanation for why we find philosophy as a site of rivalry and war and why even a radical left-wing philosopher like Deleuze could find a way to excuse Greek tyrants. According to Laruelle such agon and rivalry is not the sign of immanence, but of vulnerability and a structural fragility: "A philosophy only attacks another because this [critique of another philosophy] – and indeed the next – is intrinsically fragile and dependent on a transcendent experience, auto-positional by philosophical delegation and *at once* chosen from among others without essential reason. The cause and the complement of this internal weakness is evidently 'philosophical faith'."[38]

The structural inability of philosophy to demythologize itself is built into the assumed universality of its reach, that is its philosophical faith. And the mythological scope of its claim to universality is built upon a fundamental confusion of yet another division producing yet another dyad. As Laruelle writes, "The supposed 'universality' of philosophy gives place to the worst misunderstandings. It is not its universality that is dubious, it is its restrained character of 'abstract' generality (metaphysics as 'abstraction' of its objects), thus of partially empirical 'generality' that appears too strict or too limited when it is measured by what the vision-in-One tolerates. Philosophical universality, as we know, is double or divided: at once *generality* and *totality*."[39] We find then that the universality of philosophy is said in two different ways. The first, "generality," is philosophy's claim to speak in some sense about everything. Philosophy is able to code shift, moving from one form of human knowledge to another, though often restricting itself in a manner that leads us to the second way in which it is said. That second way, "totality," is often the form of universality that is too limited, however counterintuitive that may sound. For what philosophy often does in its code shifting is aim to unite the discourses under a single unitary discourse, thereby erasing one for the other.

In distinction, then, like Horkheimer and Adorno who in part reach for a reconnection of abstract science with the practical world, Laruelle instead suggests that the cure to philosophy's counterfeit universality is greater abstraction: "Philosophy is not too 'abstract': it is still not abstract enough, or is only 'abstracted' from experience and has not known how to liberate itself sufficiently enough to maintain with experience freer relations of a pure transcendental thought finding in the empirical nothing but a simple occasion and some support."[40] So non-philosophy will aim for an abstraction that operates in a different register than philosophy's abstraction. Instead of claiming simply to be abstracted from the empirical realm, it will be a truly free transcendental (or, in Laruelle's current terminology, "immanental") thought. It is in this sense that non-philosophy wants to retain something of the universal: "This is why non-philosophy announces itself from the outset as a universalization, *of the 'non-Euclidean' type* if you will, of the philosophical generality/totality."[41] That is, a universalization of thought, where the ways it may productively enter into relation with wider practices is extended, in a further generalization of philosophy without any attempt at creating or representing a totality. It is here that

Laruelle's non-philosophy may be productively coupled with work done in critical theory around race and gender, for non-philosophy shares in the project of limiting *European* philosophy's claims to represent a truly *generic* form of thought. It may enter into such generality, but only by first recognizing that it will have to itself be transformed, perhaps even past recognition, by "going under" (in the sense of "going under anesthesia" and not submission) the condition that European philosophy too must become a material and so merely a relative practice in such a generic form of thought with a proliferation of such relative practices.

The dualysis then not only allows for Laruelle's creation of a kind of non-mythology as I have tried to sketch here, but also allows for what he calls the "real critique of pure reason." This critique means taking the philosophical projection of Reason (with a capital R) and placing it under real conditions, meaning under the conditions of unilateral duality that show Reason precisely as something projected by philosophy in a halluci-natory form *and* also having some real identity that is not simply an itera-tion of itself. From this Laruelle is able to see how Reason is an instance of the force-(of)-thought, for reason does something: "According to non-philosophical 'logic', we say that the force-(of)-thought is the *non-rational* identity of Reason, and consequently that it unifies-it-without-totalizing-it."[42] To say then that this is "non-rational" is to make a claim analogous to the "non-mythology" created, that is, that this vision of reason finds itself freed from the hallucinatory power of Reason (again, with the capital R intended). As Laruelle writes, "The non-rational is not the opposite or the margin of philosophy. The non-rational is the *theoretical usage* or identity of Reason, itself always impure or empirico-rational, under the cause-of-the-last-instance that is the vision-in-One. The 'non' limits Reason to its identity-of-the-last-instance and tears it from philosophy, universalizing it beyond its philosophical forms which all *share it* between generality and totality."[43] In this way, reason is both limited and freed, something may be created and yet the power of reason will not be allowed to overrun the identity of a human being. Against certain philosophies that seek to unbind reason so that it may have its way with human beings, destroying them in the name of some higher and more valued rationality that humans are meant to serve so that reason may go beyond them, reason is cast by non-philosophy as relative to the lived reality of humans, thereby freeing those very humans-in-person from the harassment of Reason. That is, instead of submitting human beings to reason, reason is submitted to the identity it is given by human beings and so "ceases to be auto-examiner and auto-limiter, tribunal for its claims."[44] For humans are the Real and so Reason as projected by philosophy simply cannot capture them since reason is a matter of measure, presentation, and representation. In so far as Reason is subject to the Real, it is subject to something beyond and foreclosed to Reason. As Laruelle writes, "The Real is more like Kant's 'thing-in-itself': unknowable and even unthinkable, but with the difference that it is not so from transcendence but from immanence (the One and not the Other) foreclosed and that it consists in an experience or a knowing of the third type, the vision-in-One."[45] The vision-in-One is a kind of mutation of philosophy that amounts to seeing something without reference to its transcendent form, it amounts to a kind of giving up on totality, to acting out something like the "lived-without-life" and "without-death."

NEITHER DEAD NOR LIVING: NON-PHILOSOPHY'S FIRST TERMS AND RECASTING THE A PRIORI

What is often shocking for readers of Laruelle is the relentless focus on and seemingly worshipful reverence for the Real. In *The Century* Alain Badiou described twentieth-century philosophy as having a "passion for the real." While he may have had Laruelle in mind here he does not mention him, relegating any engagement to a passing footnote where he points the reader with some disdain to Laruelle's critique of decision, a practice that Badiou himself champions as a source of philosophy's power.[46] Yet, it may not merely have been disdain that kept Badiou from engaging directly with Laruelle. For in Badiou's diagnosis the passion for the real is a passion to uncover masks and get to the reality underneath. This may manifest itself in at least two different ways: 1) as a focus on identity and authenticity, or 2) in the construction of an axiomatic that would allow for the measuring of the difference between true and false. Badiou prefers the second, since the first prizes destruction in the name of a purity that can never be finally reached, whereas the second avoids the trap of an illusory purity by casting the real as a gap between truth and simulacrum, instead of an identity beneath a mask.[47] Laruelle's axiomatic sense of the Real is similar to Badiou's in that it is not an "identity" that a philosopher or anyone else can reach through the process of reduction and destruction of the inauthentic, the untrue, the simulacrum, or whatever term is cast as the obverse of the presumed real identity. But, unlike Badiou, Laruelle's Real does not allow for an axiomatic measuring of the Real. The Real remains foreclosed even to the axioms formed around it and that form the practice of non-philosophy. The appeal to measurement by Badiou is an appeal to decision, literally to decide where the gap is between real and unreal, the true and the false. For Badiou, the purpose of this decision is to bear witness to truths that emerge through events or in "evental sites" outside of philosophy (science, politics, art, and love), but which only philosophy can give voice to the veracity of. One may see this as a thinly veiled will to power, whereas

Laruelle's analysis of decision is a pragmatics of thought that aims at doing something with philosophy, without needing to be recognized as the one who speaks for philosophy or any regional forms of knowing.

This is then ultimately what is at work in the concept of "first names" that Laruelle deploys and explains in this chapter. Where Heidegger and Sartre aimed to "destroy" (according to Badiou), and Badiou aims to "subtract," Laruelle aims to "clone," and one form such clones take is these first names. He writes:

> The transcendental axiomatization of conceptual language or philosophical discourse equalizes, but in the mode of the "last instance", the *first term* (necessary for axiomatization) and the *proper name* (every language must be reduced to "speak" the Real('s)-identity or to receive a transcendental function) under the form of *first name*. [...] This is the end of philosophical "ventriloquism"; language speaks from the immanent phenomenon to which it is reduced through-and-through.[48]

The philosophical terms that proliferate and are distributed in the language of philosophical texts are not the immanent phenomenon they stand in for (though this is speaking generally, since formal logic is not the same as ordinary language). For Laruelle these terms are now transformed into simple first names that speak only from the Real, without any claim to speak of the Real or to decide upon their own truth or validity.

This leads us to our final example of a dualysis at work in *Principles of Non-Philosophy*: the dualysis of life. Here we return to the work of Michel Henry and his phenomenology that privileges life as a term for radical immanence. As already touched upon in earlier chapters, Henry's radical phenomenology is taken by Laruelle as a forerunner of his own non-philosophy, and even obliquely credited as a radicalization of Husserlian and Heideggerian forms of phenomenology with their focus on the *Erlebnis* or "lived experience," but one which remains thoroughly enchained by philosophical faith. In Henry's case, philosophical faith is present in his casting life as the true locus of the Real's authenticity, as a concept that exists a priori to all other forms of thinking and even to philosophy itself, even though philosophy may come to think it. It is this use of an a priori term that threatens the use of first names in non-philosophy and threatens to make of the non-philosopher simply another braggart boasting of her unique abilities to defeat all other philosophers in philosophical battle:

> The danger of this appearance is the greatest for this class of symbols which refer explicitly to the real-One or which enter into the axioms charged with describing it. It is in this manner that non-philosophy can lose its rigor and turn to a new philosophy: to the metaphysical thesis of the determination of

the Real through thought. Hence the hope of its direct definition through the first names of Life, Affect, Internal, Impressional, or any other term which appears to have, or which has had within the metaphysical tradition, a special affinity with radical immanence and power – a divine surprise of naming – managing to finally touch the finger of the true Real ignored by other philosophies.[49]

In what should by now be a familiar move, Laruelle claims that non-philosophy may avoid this trap through recourse to the logic of the last-instance and the foreclosed nature of the Real: "The real-One allows us to understand that Life, Affect, the Originary Impression or the Internal, etc., are real in-the-last-instance and that, precisely because of this, they are not the Real but only – given their constitution as symbols – the first terms which describe it without determining it."[50] It is here that the reader may begin to understand the use that Laruelle makes of the Kantian notion of the a priori. For the nature of the first names he deploys is to locate certain a priori elements at play within philosophy (not, it is important to note, within the lived nature of the Lived). These first terms – which emerge via the process of dualyzing standard philosophical concepts, ideas, and structures – can be understood as taking the a priori elements of philosophical mixtures and deploying them in a more direct, unilateral form. What must be done to bring this unilateral form out? The self-sufficient, transcendent, and hallucinatory elements of the concept must be stripped out. But this would not be sufficient for the creation of new forms of knowing, since knowing requires something of a relative transcendence in the form of what Laruelle calls a transcendental appearance. Another way to think of the transcendental appearance is to connect it to Laruelle's conception of a priori and first names, since they are what will determine certain relative creations, new considerations of the problem of living and dying for example, without claiming to determine the Real or the One. The transcendental or a priori appearance is what must take place as a rethinking and recasting of philosophy's hallucinations of these terms as absolutely transcendent. They must be recast as relative and so as in some sense material; even symptoms are material to be worked with for the diagnostician, and hallucinations are tools productive for great artists. As long as the thinking is productive without allowing its production to stand in for the Real, then it is non-philosophy: "The problem of thought as force-(of)-thought – precisely the sense of this substitution – is of thinking rigorously and in reality the sphere of ontico-ontological givens of philosophy under the conditions of the vision-in-One, rather than of thinking the vision-in-One under the conditions of philosophy."[51]

To unpack this by way of an example we will now turn to the summary of Laruelle's dualysis of Henry's conception of life. I will first quote the section in full before offering a commentary that will return to certain lines:

> The mechanism of this transcendental appearance can be outlined in the following manner. Let us assume that the Real is named in the register of "life", the "lived", in the phenomenological manner. The first term which corresponds to it must thus simultaneously detach it from life in its psycho-metaphysical senses. We thus form the first name of the *lived-without-life*, a manner of radicalizing the phenomenological *Erlebnis*. But this is insufficient: this name only has a transcendental status. The Real itself has nothing to do with life or even the lived, it is only immanent-(to)-itself (therefore nothing to do with a metaphysical or phenomenological immanence, etc.), without particular ontico-ontological determination. The lived, even "without-life", remains a simple symbol that does not *approach* the real-One at all in an asymptotic manner: adequacy excludes approximation. Simply put it is possible to speak the Real (this term itself is a first name) with the means of "life". But this does not permit us to conclude from the name to the thing.[52]

We first see Laruelle locate the field from which the object of his dualysis will be pulled: the aforementioned radical phenomenology of life that Henry pursued. Laruelle must then locate the specific way in which the Real is named in that field, which in this case is found in the register of "life" or simply "the lived." When Laruelle claims that the concept must be detached "simultaneously [...] from life in its psycho-metaphysical senses" he is following Henry's radical move to think life under the phenomenological epoche or via the bracketing of any semblance of the natural attitude that covers over the pure manifestation of life, the manifestation without any mediation:

> What is manifest is manifestation itself. [...] And in fact biology never encounters life, knows nothing of it, has not the slightest idea of it. When by some extraordinary circumstance it is biology itself that speaks – biology and not a biologist who is imbued with the ideals or prejudices of his time – it pronounces a sentence on itself, declares truthfully and lucidly what it is: *"Biologists no longer study life today."* We must take it at its word: *in biology there is no life, there are only algorithms.*[53]

Readers will already see where Laruelle diverges from Henry, most notably with regard to the latter's outright contempt for the sciences. For Laruelle sees here an instance of philosophy's transcendental mythology at play, its attempt to cast philosophy itself as what has unique access to the Real. In order to take phenomenological bracketing to its radical conclusion philosophy as metaphysics must itself be bracketed. Laruelle symbolizes this with the term "lived-without-life" and claims it as a further radicalization of phenomenology's guiding concept of *Erlebnis* (usually translated into French as *vécu* and into English as "lived experience," as discussed already in Chapter 2). Importantly, and as we might expect, Laruelle declares that such a non-philosophical name remains insufficient, meaning that the term is deployed with the understanding that it has a kind of weak or relative force – it does work, but it is not the totality of work itself. It is a kind of "worked-upon-without-work," to follow the non-philosophical formulation. These first names allow the science of non-philosophy to engage with philosophy: "The symbols as 'lived-without-life', 'given-without-givenness', etc., are symbols *for* philosophy but not symbols *of* philosophy and still less knowledge *of the* Real."[54] The contrast with standard philosophical practice, as Laruelle sees it, is important. Standard philosophy creates concepts that are said to model reality, or what Laruelle would claim is a hallucinated Real. In the case of Henry, his phenomenology of life finds what life is in itself and then reads all other phenomena through the lens of what it claims is manifest in itself. In a certain sense Henry sees his philosophy as living by virtue of its taking part in the absolute form of life he has identified. Another philosopher, Ray Brassier (to pick an example of someone whose early work was friendly to Laruelle's but inimical to Henry's), claims instead to identify the ultimate *telos* or end of all life in annihilation as the very condition which philosophy must set itself under. In a perfectly convertible way, we find the nihilist philosopher following the same philosophical logic as the Christian philosopher:

> if everything is dead already, this is not only because extinction disables those possibilities which were taken to be constitutive of life and existence, but also because the will to know is driven by the traumatic reality of extinction, and strives to become equal to the trauma of the in-itself whose trace it bears. In becoming equal to it, philosophy achieves a binding of extinction, through which the will to know is finally rendered commensurate with the in-itself. This binding coincides with the objectification of thinking understood as the *adequation without correspondence* between the objective reality of extinction and the subjective knowledge of the trauma to which it gives rise. It is this adequation that constitutes the truth of extinction. But to acknowledge this truth, the subject of philosophy must also recognize that he or she is already dead, and that philosophy is neither a medium of affirmation nor a source of justification, but rather the organon of extinction.[55]

Brassier, being an adept reader and an important early advocate of the *philosophical* value of Laruelle's work, does not shy away from doing philosophy in an explicitly standard mode.[56] And it is all there: extinction or annihilation identified as the locus and condition of thought under which all thinking must submit itself. While they may appear very unlike one another, since Henry excises science but privileges religion and Brassier excises religion and privileges science, the reality is that both choose to totally excise a form of knowing from philosophical practice while submitting their privileged dialogue partner to a version that is utterly determined by their philosophy.

These instances of life (for Henry) and death (for Brassier) are both a prioris for different *philosophical* discourses. The term a priori is familiar to readers of post-Kantian philosophy precisely because of the central place that Kant's critical philosophy, especially in the *Critique of Pure Reason*, gives to delineating the relationship of experience and pure reason (that is, what reason can do with certainty prior to experience). The term is shorthand for judgments of reason that are made "prior to experience" and is contrasted with those that are "a posteriori" or judgments made "after experience." The classic example of an a priori judgment given in introductory philosophy courses is "all bachelors are unmarried," since the definition of bachelor is to be an unmarried man. Something akin to "some bachelors are unhappy" is a typical example of an a posteriori judgment, which requires experience of both happiness and bachelors before the judgment can be made. Kant's philosophy made certain universal claims about reason in the World, so to speak, and so his sense of the a priori is a claim about reason and experience as such. Laruelle's sense of the a priori does not concern the structures of the human mind, or transcendental reason, or the structures of the universe. Instead, the a priori is relativized and refers to each philosophy and what structures its deployment into the realms of experience. With Henry it is a matter of life and with Brassier it is a matter of death, as what structures and determines the rest of their philosophical utterances. It is important to note that while this use of the a priori is very important in *Principles of Non-Philosophy*, it does not recur often and is not included in the *Dictionary of Non-Philosophy*, written as a kind of companion volume to *Principles of Non-Philosophy*. The a priori appears to operate in much the same way as "first names" do in other texts and in some sense might even be a first name derived from those Kantian and post-Kantian philosophies that are used as materials throughout *Principles of Non-Philosophy*.[57] In this way, Laruelle's use of the a priori is closer to Michel Foucault's in *The Order of Things* than it is to Kant's in the *Critique of Pure Reason*. For Foucault looked at the way in which certain "historical a prioris" structured what he called "epistemes" or the conditions for knowledge in one epoch as compared with another.[58] Laruelle, unlike Foucault and so in this way closer to Kant, does not use the a priori in a purely historical way or in a way that is determined by historical factors, but as an ahistorical, invariant part of the structure of any philosophy at all. We may summarize the a priori then as local, in so far as it is always attached to a philosophy that is relative to the Real, but also as transcendental (or immanental), in so far as it structures that relative philosophy in a radical way regardless of the materials that philosophy aims to intervene within.

Philosophy always offers an absolute choice. But what choice does it really give except what master to sit under, what absolute to serve? What choice does it demand we make that is not at bottom a choice about which mythology we are going to blind ourselves to? The non-philosophical method is designed to engage with these choices, but to not choose; to delineate the borders and shapes of decisions, but without ever giving over to an absolute decision. It is, in a certain sense, a promiscuous and clandestine form of thought, willing to engage with any form of knowledge and thereby create something of it and the spontaneous and unacknowledged philosophy often tarrying with it. Yet it can only do so because it refuses the hallucinatory determination of its language. It refuses to submit to anything determinate and represented, like life or extinction, living or dying. As a method it can only be practiced faithfully through simply being immanent-(to)-itself, as manifest-without-manifestation. Readers of Laruelle will often find this kind of formulation, where the past participle comes to act as a substantive instead of the usual nominal case. This is what is at play in concepts like the lived-without-life. Thus the language of non-philosophy is a language derived from philosophy, but transformed into a form of thinking driven by a pragmatics of the now rather than metaphysical determination.[59] What Laruelle claims of non-philosophical language is true of dualysis more generally: "it only exists in these two modes belonging to it insofar as it is *lived*, neither dead nor living, but lived-in-the-last-instance-without-life."[60] That is, the only way dualysis occurs is through the practice of dualysis, the outcome of which is as undetermined as the lived (reality) of one's own life.[61]

6

The Stranger, Nowhere at Home: Non-Philosophy and the Philosophical Scene

Here in the final chapter I must beg the reader's indulgence. Guides become tired, even when they are just pointing out shapes in the sky. For as you strain to make the points of light appear in some intelligible shape, so too is the guide straining to tell the story of those constellations. Or, if we've moved from simply stargazing to exploring, the guide also tires as he directs those following over difficult terrain. As that terrain is worked over the guide hopes the map is leading the others in something like the right direction, but of course there are other vectors and other paths one could have taken and so the responsibility towards those following the proclaimed guide weighs heavy.

For most of us in the Anglophone world when we are first taught philosophy it comes relatively late in life. For people like me, products of a public school system in the United States, it was not until my first year of university. Some others may have been lucky enough, through birth or circumstance, to find themselves being taught Plato or Descartes in high school, though of course some of these ideas trickle down to us through the plots of films and other artistic forms of the force-(of)-thought. But that moment when you first sit before a teacher, a guide of sorts, who, if they're still not jaded by the school system, tries to convince you to follow, to see how far the rabbit hole goes, is often a moment where one is caught between childhood and adulthood, between wonder and cynicism. And the offer made to you is that you don't have to choose. That you can chase truth, you can be seduced by it, you can sit beneath a tree and think about truth, beauty, and goodness. Moreover, that what those terms may end up meaning may lead you to see them in things like death, decay, and the most egregious forms of evil. That is, you are invited to think a tradition that begins with Plato and, though it has not ended with Levinas or Adorno, must at least pass through the Holocaust as a new a priori for thought. So, there is something promised to you from Plato to twentieth-century European philosophy. I know it tempted me, and though attention to suffering means that the Holocaust may no longer be taken as the universal a priori (as thinkers as divergent as Badiou and Frantz Fanon have argued it cannot), philosophy still offered me a way to attend to suffering within thought.

But where can one cash in such a promissory note? Can the promise of philosophy ever be delivered upon? The promise of philosophy is more philosophy. It is a promise that upon undertaking philosophy one will have undertaken philosophy. It is not a general equivalent. It will not allow you to exchange one good for another. In a certain sense, philosophy is a form of money that exists to reproduce itself. So Plato's dialogues beget books on Plato. Even forms of philosophy less attentive to historical issues do not provide the object of their study, but another text delineating and mediating that object in a way which determines the way it is then taken within thought. And of course, unconcerned as I am regarding charges of hypocrisy, it should be noted that this book on non-philosophy is one that aims not simply to be a mirror, but is nonetheless a book which is begotten by another book.

Regarding humanity, Nietzsche rhetorically asks in his *Genealogy of Morality*: "To breed an animal with the prerogative to *promise* – is that not precisely the paradoxical task which nature has set herself with regard to humankind?"[1] Whether or not "nature" is to bear the responsibility of producing the promise of humankind and its philosophies or these are simply the product of philosophical hallucinations within philosophical hallucinations is not the issue here. But perhaps the foolishness of making such a promise is forgiven by non-philosophy through the systematic unveiling of its faith in itself. Instead of limiting knowledge to make room for faith, as Kant did in his *Critique of Pure Reason*, Laruelle instead limits faith to making room for lived knowing. Instead of the promises of philosophy as transcendental mythology, we are given now the prospect of building with a philosophy disempowered but still teeming with potentiality as simple materials.

If non-philosophy makes a promise, it does so without any authority and without being a recognized currency. Instead, it creates heretical identities and discourses, it creates unified theories and not networks:

> Non-Philosophy is the matrix of disciplines of the type called "unified theories" which each time manifest the "simple" a priori correlation of philosophy and a region. They are specified by the regional materials whereas their designation

as "first" (in the sense of a priority-without-primacy) designates the place of philosophy within the materials and of the transcendental within non-philosophy: First Science, First Ethics, First Technology or Aesthetics, etc.[2]

So, as we can see from what Laruelle has written, whatever promise non-philosophy makes is written on the back of philosophical texts, technical manuals, books of poetry and fiction, scientific studies, and the like.

This final chapter will take a different form than the preceding. If the other chapters have traced the influences and the shape of concepts, this chapter sets aside the impossible task of guiding the reader through the massive final chapter of *Principles of Non-Philosophy*. I have set aside such a task not only because "The Constitution of the Non-Philosophical Order" is too long to be traced in a single chapter (it runs to just over seventy pages in the translation and is broken up into four distinct sections which could constitute four distinct chapters of their own), but also because the concepts traced and unpacked throughout this book are largely the same ones at work in the final chapter. As this book was never intended to be a substitute for the original text it is commenting upon, the reader should now have a strong understanding of the main concepts required for working through the final chapter. For "The Constitution of the Non-Philosophical Order" may be read as a summary of the entire *Principles of Non-Philosophy* shorn of the references and examples that frame the rest of the text. The rest of the book explains the conditions for non-philosophy's hypothesis, while this chapter aims to outline the actual domain itself.[3] So, in this final chapter of the introduction and guide, I will instead provide a reading of how non-philosophy's delineation of its domain situates the method of non-philosophy within the post-Kantian, post-phenomenological milieu in which it was written and within contemporary philosophy as practiced today, nearly twenty years after *Principles of Non-Philosophy* was written. The goal of this exercise is to help those readers who want to know what promise there may be in non-philosophy for helping them in their own thinking, and how it may help to think through certain problems of thought that arise in philosophical work and within domains that do not quite count as such for the university discourse of philosophy.

LARUELLE AND (POST-)CONTINENTAL PHILOSOPHY

There is a familiar though misguided critique of French philosophy that reigns in Anglophone philosophy departments to the effect that it is all "fashionable nonsense." That is, nonsense compared to the apparently clear-headed work of asking, "What is it like to be a bat?," or to yet again ask students in ethics classes to consider whether they would push a "fat man" in front of a trolley to stop it, thereby murdering him but preventing the killing of five other people. Such questions do not strike me as the model of clarity, setting aside the question of whether or not clarity should guide the project of critical thought when it means simply something like "common sense." The ideology in favor of "clarity" reigns despite it being far from conceptually clear what is meant by it. One need only to open a book of analytic metaphysics to know that technical language or "jargon" is used there too, and moreover that such technical language has a purpose behind it. Of course, one may be cynical about Continental philosophy as well, since oftentimes the debates seem to be about whether Hegel is simply right about everything or only mostly right. When surveying the contemporary scene of philosophy, whether Team Continental or Team Analytic, it is sometimes difficult to find the value in it or a good reason that it should continue in this anemic form. Some think that it has taken this form because philosophy as such has dissolved into particular sciences that are able to answer philosophical questions in ways that philosophy is simply unable to. This dissolution is one way to understand the proclamation that we have reached "the end of philosophy," a proclamation that rang out in the lands of Continental and analytic philosophy. Many readers who appear to have only skimmed Laruelle's texts, whether in English or their original French, have lumped Laruelle under this banner, making him another voice in the din regarding the death or end of philosophy. Non-Philosophy does not make this proclamation though, and does not in its mature form claim that science has some unique access to the Real or that philosophy is falling away as greater sciences take on the tasks it once had. For there is in each of these sciences and regional forms of knowledge a spontaneous form of philosophy, of self-sufficiency, which will require disempowering through a science of philosophy which non-philosophy constitutes.

So, importantly, Laruelle does not declare philosophy's decline, death, or end. Laruelle incessantly says so himself, and is forced to make this constant declaration since so many of his critics continue to make this mistake. To take but one example, in *Philosophy and Non-Philosophy* he writes, "Non-Philosophy is not the overwhelming negation of philosophy, its (impossible) deconstruction, but another usage, *the only one that can be defined outside its spontaneous belief in itself, a practice of philosophy which is no longer founded and enclosed in philosophical faith but is positively established within the limits of the bracketing of this faith.*"[4] In this passage, beyond the seemingly negative project, we see non-philosophy for the constructive project it really is. And it is in fact a wildly constructive project, as evidenced by Laruelle's work spanning ethics, philosophy of religion and theology, epistemology and philosophy of science, political philosophy, and aesthetics. It is able to be wildly productive by virtue of bracketing philosophical faith, that is the faith in philosophy and its sufficiency, opening it to new mutations and permutations, new iterations and codes, in a pragmatic of human force. Standard philosophy is a priestly endeavor. It is always mediating between the human subject and the so-called real object or between regional knowing and the truth of that knowing. Non-Philosophy is thought lived. But this lived form of thinking is not spontaneous, nor is it uncritical. There is, to call upon the title of the last chapter in *Principles of Non-Philosophy*, an order to non-philosophy. This order is precisely the establishment or discovery of the limits to the bracketing of philosophical faith; at once a disempowering of philosophy's self-sufficient faith and a tracing of the power or potential inherent within philosophy still. But if Laruelle is forced to play the philosophers' game – and he is an Emeritus Professor of Contemporary Philosophy and taught in philosophy departments his entire career – then of course he is going to be assumed to play on "Team Continental." He is part of a tradition of radical philosophy in France that has at times been appropriated in the Anglophone world under the vague title "French Theory." This includes thinkers who were trained as philosophers but went on to do the kind of work that starts to make the academic border police nervous, like Jacques Derrida, Pierre Bourdieu, Luce Irigaray, and Michel Foucault, but may at times also include thinkers who are clearly philosophers and are such in a very classical style, like Gilles Deleuze, Michel Henry, and Alain Badiou.

What does it mean, though, to place Laruelle within the Continental tradition? Well, first, following John Ó Maoilearca, we should admit that, "'Philosophically' speaking [...] there is no such thing as 'Continental philosophy' *per se* – this is both a sham geo-cultural distinction and a category error."[5] In so far as Laruelle is French and was trained in philosophy through the French academia, then he deploys vocabulary and methods which arise out of Continental philosophy, though even there we mean specifically German and French philosophy. Laruelle himself even says so: "What is an act of philosophical thinking? Of course, I respond to that question with my own resources, so-called 'Continental' and not 'analytic' ones."[6] But as Ó Maoilearca goes on to write:

> There is not one philosophical theme that is exclusive to the European continent, nor any outside the continent that is confined to 'Anglo-American' philosophy. The use of the term 'continental' also brings to mind its other ill-coined associate, 'analytic philosophy'; but no methodological barrier exists between the two traditions either. In fact, it is extremely difficult to make any distinction stand up under historical, methodological or philosophical scrutiny.[7]

111

In a certain sense, then, to locate Laruelle as a Continental philosopher is simply to place him within a particular kind of ecosystem of thought.[8] Theoretically there is no reason why the methods of non-philosophy could not be used on so-called analytic philosophy just as much as they have been used to think through German Idealism, phenomenology, and deconstruction. But, seeing as the borders, artificial thought they may be, are securely placed in the world of academia there would be little encouragement from the mainstream of analytic or Anlgophone philosophy to pursue such a research program.

What does it mean, then, to place Laruelle here amongst the Continentals? Well, in part it names a certain kind of understanding of knowledge as mediated between "science" and "poetry" (and I place these in scare quotes precisely because in some sense they are philosophical hallucinations). That is, as Simon Critchley claims, Continental philosophy is a certain attempt to deal with the gap *felt* (as an existential, political, and social problem) between knowledge and wisdom.[9] Again, this is not to claim that what is increasingly misnamed analytic philosophy is unconcerned with such questions, though perhaps they are not at the heart of the project, and the resources present in contemporary analytic philosophy are not deployed in Laruelle's own construction of his non-philosophy (it is important to note, however, that the work of Wittgenstein, Gödel, and to a limited extent Bertrand Russell, three touchstones for analytic philosophers, are vital). James Burton identifies three dominant models in Continental philosophy marked by the proper names Derrida, Badiou, and Deleuze. Laruelle has written on all three of these contemporaries, and though he has not characterized their philosophies in exactly the way Burton does, Burton's explication does help us to understand the milieu Laruelle's non-philosophy emerges from. For Burton, Derrida's philosophy is concerned with the "possibility of the impossible" or the ways in which certain impossibilities, like "access to the real beyond *logos*," drive and structure philosophy.[10] Badiou, situated as a kind of inverse of Derrida by Burton, is instead concerned with the "possibility of philosophy" where such a possibility is predicated on the existence of the production of truth outside of philosophy itself. Badiou's understanding of philosophy limits its role to a certain meta-relationship, so that for example the domain of ontology is really the purview of mathematics while philosophy performs a kind of meta-ontology akin to the metamathematics Gödel laid out.[11] Finally, Deleuze is presented by Burton as paradigmatic of "concept creation" or as a movement within thought that is not progressive in a homogeneous sense, but moves in a heterogeneous fashion, with fits and starts. Here the concern is no longer with possibility or impossibility, but with a kind of healthy-minded pragmatics of thought unconcerned with philosophy's ultimate place within the cosmos.

Of course, Burton is not making a naive or overly simplistic point, and he goes on to speak about the thousand exceptions to these three models. However, though Laruelle's non-philosophy is not easily placed within these three methods, it should not be treated as one of the exceptions. Instead, it may mark a kind of identity of the three disempowered of any single claim to sufficiency. As in Derrida there is a certain kind of "impossibility" driving non-philosophy, this being the foreclosure of the One-Real to philosophy, which drives non-philosophy by relativizing philosophy itself and disempowering the faith in philosophy. As in Badiou non-philosophy requires that philosophy be combined with some other regional knowing, though unlike Badiou, Laruelle does not arbitrarily limit this to four domains (art, politics, science, and love) nor does he then proceed to pass judgment on what gets to count as an event within those domains. Finally, as in Deleuze, there is a certain wild pragmatics at play in non-philosophy, as it aims to create new forms of knowing through its construction of unified theories. If Burton's typology of methods in Continental philosophy is correct, then the potential in Laruelle's non-philosophy is in part as a method that may allow us to disempower the promise of Continental philosophy but at the same time build with it to bridge the gap between wisdom and knowledge in allowing for a kind of discourse that is scientific, ethical, political, religious, artistic, and philosophical all at once.

SPECULATIVE REALISM AND THE NON-SPECULAR REAL

What goes under the name of Continental philosophy does not only apply to philosophy done in Germany, France, and elsewhere on the European continent, and so this form of philosophy does not come to an end with the philosophies of Derrida, Badiou, and Deleuze. In recent years the focus in Continental philosophy has drifted from the poststructuralist and deconstructionist "end of metaphysics" to a return of metaphysics in various guises. Some have marked this as a turn to Continental philosophy taking the mathematical and physical sciences seriously, though the veracity of this claim is historically dubious. But undoubtedly, for a younger generation of readers within or coming out of Continental philosophy there has been something of a shift towards the metaphysics of naturalism, materialism, and/or realism. Anglophone interest in Laruelle's non-philosophy originally centered around those interested in the "speculative turn," or philosophers grouped under the name of "speculative realism."

This nascent movement is usually thought to originate around a critique of what Quentin Meillassoux calls "correlationism." In his *After Finitude* he defines correlationism in this way: "By 'correlation' we mean the idea according to which we only ever have access to the correlation between thinking and being, and never to either term considered apart from the other. We will henceforth call correlationism any current of thought which maintains the unsurpassable character of the correlation so defined."[12] In a certain sense what Laruelle critiques in philosophy is something like correlationism. The basic critique of philosophy that Laruelle puts forward is that it believes itself sufficient to think the Real – philosophy confuses some particular aspect of its own construction as sufficient to determine the Real itself. And here the Real comes to stand in for a host of concepts, but what it really means is "the thing-in-itself," not the thing-in-itself as understood ontologically, but understood through the thing itself. Thus, if we were to put this in the idiom of Meillassoux, there is a correlation between philosophy or thought and the Real. Yet Laruelle's response to this, as we have seen, is not like Meillassoux's in *After Finitude*. Meillassoux separates out primary and secondary qualities such that there is a true quality of the thing-in-itself that it is possible to know mathematically, and a secondary quality that is added on to the object through human subjectivity. For Laruelle the problem here is one of the relationship between the subject and the object, as in Meillassoux, but one where this relationship is seen as a kind of philosophical dualism and mixture that actually is related unilaterally to the Real that relates to both subject and object as projections or philosophical hallucinations. We have seen how this works formally around the schema of the One.

Despite this similarity it would be a mistake to call non-philosophy speculative realism *avant la lettre*.[13] In fact, Meillassoux does not describe his work as a speculative realism, but (at least in *After Finitude*) as a speculative materialism. The name "speculative realism" is something of a historical accident, and the usefulness of the term as a descriptor is as debatable as the lasting importance of the work grouped under it.[14] Without entering into debates regarding the origin of the term we may quickly note that it was originally simply the name for a conference featuring the work of Ray Brassier (who we have seen was one the first Anglophone readers and promoters of Laruelle's work, but who has since marked a distance from the larger claims of non-philosophy), Quentin Meillassoux, Graham Harman, and Iain Hamilton Grant. The proceedings of this conference were published in the independent, avant-garde philosophy journal *Collapse*, popular amongst a disparate group of young philosophy students who communicated online through blogs and other social media. Owing in part to the speed with which conversations take place online, the four original "speculative realists" quickly acquired for students a hallowed status that would previously have needed to be mediated by the gatekeepers of academic philosophy. And as the readers of these four began to notice the great differences between their various philosophies, battle lines were drawn and territories marked.

Various online sub-groups began to appear, grouped together under the general heading of speculative realism, and for those gathered around the nihilistic rationalism of Brassier there was an assumption that, because he had made use of Laruelle, non-philosophy could be grouped there as well. Others, Graham Harman amongst them, wanted to deny the brand name to Laruelle. Regardless of the merits or shortcomings of Harman's object-oriented philosophy (and I do not claim any position on that here), his method of reading the history of philosophy and of assessing contemporary philosophy is marked by metaphors of mastery and marketing. It is his notion I am following here when I refer to "speculative realism" as a brand:

> The phrase "speculative realism" is no longer beloved by everyone it describes, and may be used less often in the future. I still find it to be an effective term, one that draws wide attention to a fairly diverse set of philosophical programmes by pointing accurately to key similarities among them. Though it is always a badge of honour for intellectuals to refuse being stamped with any sort of label, other fields of human innovation have a much stronger sense for the value of a brand name. The brand is not merely a degenerate practice of brainwashing consumerism, but a universally recognized method of conveying information while cutting through information clutter. Coining specific names for philosophical positions helps orient the intellectual public on the various available options while also encouraging untested permutations. If the decision were mine alone, not only would the name "speculative realism" be retained, but a logo would be designed for projection on PowerPoint screens, accompanied by a few signature bars of smoky dubstep music. It is true that such practices would invite snide commentary about "philosophy reduced to marketing gimmicks".[15]

While Harman has – somewhat mercifully – not followed up this threat to create a logo and compose some "smoky dubstep," he has attempted to exercise a kind of copyright control against claims that Laruelle is part of "speculative realism."[16] It is important to recognize that the term has come to be used in reference to thinkers outside of the original four, being used to mark a whole host of thinkers who are not "realists" in any philosophically meaningful sense, and that perhaps it would be more useful, and less misleading, to follow Ó Maoilearca's earlier suggestion of marking recent creative trends in Continental philosophy as "post-Continental philosophy" or even "Continental naturalism."[17] But, while perhaps Laruelle could be included under such a post-Continental label, he has expressed no interest in being called a speculative realist nor in using the term to increase his fortunes in readership and influence as others have. In an unpublished interview with Drew S. Burk, Laruelle remarks that

> As always this expression "speculative realism" is a banner that unites various dissatisfactions and deceptions that are all extremely different without any kind of great unity. [...] I have always felt estranged from this current which is for me, it seems, marked by a metaphysical nostalgia, and I have nothing in common with them except for a shared desire to renew the philosophical decision and to exit the phenomenological era and its residual humanism, but as my own work is concerned, I want to return to the real rather than to a realism. A materiality rather than a materialism.[18]

So, let us be done with a certain kind of belonging, a certain feeling at home when those with the right brand are around. Whatever speculative realism is – and whether or not it exists – I am far more interested in the turn towards speculation and the rapprochement it has brought about between the natural sciences and a certain way of doing philosophy. For it is beyond question that this turn has, if nothing else, excited people and made them feel free in new ways ... though as every good Deleuzian knows, we should always be aware that a line of flight can become stratified and so turn into a new cage for the subjects that were passing through it. The fact is that Laruelle's non-philosophy effected this rapprochement between Continental philosophy and the sciences decades prior to the current speculative turn. He has even shown himself to be concerned with a kind of "realist" philosophy at least as far back as 1981 in his book *Le Principe de minorité*. This concern was manifest long before Harman's or Manuel DeLanda's work, even if Laruelle now has modified his claim under the demands of non-philosophical rigor into a concern for the Real rather than realism.[19] We have touched upon this relation of science and philosophy within non-philosophy, so the task before us now is to compare the project of speculative realism to non-philosophy in order to understand in a comparative way what non-philosophy can do and what it aims to do. Since there is no unity to speculative realism, I have made use of Louis Morelle's typology in his article "Speculative Realism: After Finitude and Beyond?" A quick word about this article and my use of it: First, I do not follow Morelle's specific classifications of thinkers nor am I trying to add anything to his discussions. In my estimation, whether thinker X is really a part of subset Y is not the point or the most useful aspect of Morelle's typology. What his essay does well is provide a kind of topology of positions that seem possible within the field of thought opened up by this speculative turn. And he does so helpfully through short theses. I will use these theses to discuss and compare Laruelle's non-philosophy to them.

116

Morelle begins with object-oriented ontology (another term used to refer to object-oriented philosophy by people other than Harman), writing:

OOO:
Correlationism: Every apprehension and every relation is essentially different from the object it aims at (the tree that I think is by definition different from the tree itself).

Anti-correlationism: there is no fundamental ontological difference in the relations between subject and object and the relations between objects.[20]

To this I will add that for non-philosophy there is no fundamental onto-logical difference in the relations between subject and object, but there is an identity of each of these objects that is prior to ontology and that is theo-retically significant or determining-in-the-last-instance. That is, of course, the One or the Real. For OOO, objects then come to be a common name for everything. In a sense that is spelled out in technical detail by these philosophers, it may even come to replace or radically modify the name of Being, as Morelle explains: "The domain of objects includes: physical objects (a quark) and theoretical objects (concepts), natural objects (a dog) and artificial objects (a computer), intangible objects (a multinational) and concrete objects, real objects and imaginary objects."[21] There is pretty much a fundamental agreement between OOO and non-philosophy on this point. The major insight of Laruelle's early work was that philosophy could be treated as one object amongst others, that philosophy was not to be privileged. For Laruelle all these objects are real in-the-last-instance and so materials to be worked with, but because they are real in-the-last-instance they are materials with specific identities that may limit how they are used.

One of the aspects of OOO that has consistently left me unsatisfied is the gap between its rhetoric and what it has actually produced. We are given "Latour lists" – essentially lists of random groupings of things, not unlike what we find in the lyrics to the Insane Clown Posse's "Miracles" – but what does that actually tell us about those objects except that they exist? In what way does it escape common sense or not simply fall into the natural attitude diagnosed by Husserl where we do not even think to ask the philosophical questions regarding those things? The difference between Laruelle and OOO on this point may be illustrated by way of the difference between popular "green consciousness" or environmentalism and what scientific ecology actually does. For environmentalism the primary axiom is that all things are related. A snail is related to the cosmos and grass is related to a school of fish in the ocean, or the waves of that ocean are related to the carbon molecules found in the atmosphere and so on. All is one and connected. And though this is true, it is not the whole picture. What scientific ecology does is locate the important differences between those relations, between the different objects that make up the biosphere, which actually tells us if the snail is particularly significant as an object in this particular relation to the cosmos or not. There appears to be a blindness to the issue of scale in OOO, at least in Harman's work, which is ironic owing to his own critique of Deleuze and philosophers who share aspects of his philosophy where there is a single "energy" or "flux" that subsumes objects. Within OOO all things are subsumed into the general category of "object" such that, while we are given a litany, we are rarely given an analysis beyond that litany, any deeper understanding of the life of objects or how this particular democracy functions. Whereas in non-philosophy there has been an intense focus on a particular object – namely thought in its philosophical form – and so the relation of philosophy to its world is explained, and even more seemingly corporeal things like photos and colors are examined in depth without any claim to provide the final verdict or philosophical judgment on these objects.[22]

This brings us to the nihilistic element of the speculative turn, which wants to think through the consequences of the insignificance of meaning attributed by subjects to objects. For these nihilists love "just is" brain chemicals. While love may still retain some local meaning, it is at bottom just chemicals. The truth of some phenomena *just is* something else, not the illusion it presents. But the difference added by the Continentally inflected philosophers taking up this kind of eliminativism lies in their understanding of the independence of rationality from the subjects who wield it. Morelle describes this tendency as follows:

"Normative nihilism" or transcendental nihilism:
Correlationism: There can only be knowledge and meaning within the limits specified by rationality.

Anti-Correlationism: Rationality is independent from any origin situated in subjective experience.[23]

He goes on to claim that this position includes the following features:

(a) Ordinary realism (independence of the world from the mind)
(b) Inferentialism (formal autonomy of reason)
(c) Scientific realism (the propositions produced by scientific and mathematical method genuinely inform us about the world)
(d) Eliminativism concerning experience (the contents of experience do not literally represent any real determination)
(e) Materialism (ontological priority of inorganic over organic, of matter over the living).[24]

Note that Morelle includes Laruelle's work here, but this is not accurate or at least not straightforwardly so. So for our non-philosophical version of this thesis it would look something like this, "rationality is independent from any origin situated in subjective experience, but only because the lived human is radically autonomous from any origin situated in subjective experience." So there is a major difference between a statement like the following, summarizing Ray Brassier's position, and Laruelle's: "Therefore, it passes from 'grass is not really, in itself, green,' to 'our experience of grass is only a secondary effect and foreign to grass itself.' Ultimately Brassier's anti-correlationism consists in its literal inversion: the correlate of thought is not being, but non-being."[25] For Laruelle even this secondary effect of greenness will be able to be located as *secondary*, it will be relatively autonomous as rooted in its own radical immanence. For even if something is secondary from the perspective of some outside observer, it is nonetheless actual in that moment regardless of that moment's fleeting nature or its status as relative and not absolute.

Strangely the main difference between this vision, most represented by Brassier, and Laruelle is that Brassier is still too-theological, rooting everything in a theory of value that is ultimately decided by its end, as we explored earlier. Now for Brassier, at least in his *Nihil Unbound*, that *telos* or end is that everything will eventually be nothing when the heat death of the universe comes. The philosophical conclusion derived from this speculative empiricism is that all meaning is ultimately local and so insignificant. For Laruelle this notion of death is itself secondary, it doesn't touch on the radical autonomy of the One-in-One, which *just is* lived.[26] For Laruelle the issue of meaning is ultimately itself overdetermined by the Philosophical Decision, so the claim that he makes isn't that meaning needs to be re-asserted against nihilism, but that nihilism believes its "just is" formalism sufficient to think the identity of something by ripping it out of illusion. Now Brassier in some way gets to this through his study of Laruelle's notion of determination-in-the-last-instance.[27] But we can locate the difference between the two as centered on the issue of contingency. Consider again our green grass and the foreignness of greenness to grass for Brassier. While it is true that the grass has its own identity separate from the human, its own determination-in-the-last-instance as grass, the contingent fact is that human beings do perceive it, that the relations between any observer's perception of the grass and the grass are still actual. The secondary effect of the grass simply cannot be separated out from the grass if we are going to deal with the actuality of the lived. Meaning here doesn't return as a return of the repressed, as it does in nihilism, but rather meaning is taken as contingent in a way that attempts

119

to see in that contingency something that is not merely local, something that is still significant as actual, indeed as *only* significant because of its lived actuality.

This relates in some sense to what Morelle calls the neo-vitalist strain in the speculative turn.

> Correlationism: No essential difference exists between the material and the ideal.

> Anti-correlationism: It is impossible to reduce the origin of existence to properties or determinations that are individually identifiable or can be apprehended by an experience.[28]

Again, he lists features of this position:

> (a) Platonist realism (the Idea exists just as much as thought and things),
> (b) a concept of matter as active and substantial rather than as a mere negation of form, and
> (c) relativity of the existence of singular things, commensurate with a dynamism more profound than the things themselves (Nature).[29]

Here Morelle's theses are more difficult to follow, but we may begin to understand them in the light of what Iain Hamilton Grant calls the extensity test, predicated on the notion that philosophy must be able to think the All.[30] Philosophy must, in other words, think the unthought and to do so it cannot simply think from one aspect (individual experience), but must in some sense think from the All as such, so without reference to an ideal experience. For Laruelle there is also a critique of this flattening of the material and the ideal, though instead of a flattening he calls this an amphibology and thinks that it is produced by philosophy itself. There is also a commitment to pluralism in non-philosophy, a pluralism that means Laruelle shares something with the dynamism of this neo-vitalism, but it is a dynamism that cannot simply settle with this Greek, philosophical vision of nature where everything has its place. Instead the non-philosophical thesis that goes with Morelle's two theses above might be something like: there is a commitment to materiality prior to the material of materialism and to the theory rather than the idea of idealism, but wherein there is a plurality of the dynamism of things-themselves that cannot be collapsed into an All, but is only determined-in-the-last-instance by the One.

This gets us to perhaps the main difference between Laruelle and the main tendencies within the speculative turn and it touches on a controversy that hasn't gone without comment. Namely that this speculative turn may mark a naive return to the project of metaphysics, even as it claims to take the natural sciences more seriously than philosophers in the Continental tradition have been credited for. Morelle's assessment of the turn suggests that there is no clear, concrete relationship to the sciences, as he sums up the figures representative of the speculative turn:

> Rejection of correlationism implies the truth of at least parts of modern naturalism as exemplified by Meillassoux's concept of ancestrality. The problem then becomes the same as with correlationism: what is the truth that naturalism superficially manifests? For Brassier, "naturalism" means complete materialism; for Harman, one must go beyond naturalism to reach an ontology where all levels of the world would be equally real; for Grant, nature as a power of creation and irreducible transformation becomes the absolute.[31]

And, as with non-philosophy, we may ask why we would want to commit to these forms of philosophy, or simply: why speculative realism? As Morelle himself says, "realism has a price."[32] So what is the price of speculative realism's approach to naturalism and materialism as it has developed so far? Speculative realism has been a race to see which philosophy can kill the human quickest. This stark claim is borne out by recent transformations of these philosophies into a new brand: accelerationism.[33] What is attacked is not the image of Man destroyed by Deleuze and Foucault, but the very notion of the significance of the human, in an attempt to excise the human from the creation of the World itself. We would need here a much longer meditation on the concept of the World in non-philosophy, but there is something going on in the speculative turn with regard to the World that is deeply troubling. The speculative turn, in its quest to break anthropocentrism, plunges the human beneath the waves of theory and holds it there until all movement stops.

If we are to summarize, what Laruelle has shown (along with thinkers as different as Heidegger and Badiou) is that in some sense the World is constructed. This is a very serious point. There is of course the idea of the World which is constructed theoretically, but there is also the material World constructed by the beings that make it up. The World is not simply out there, waiting to be discovered, as it sometimes seems with the recent turn towards an apolitical ontology, but in the age of ecological doom (crisis is not the right word) it seems downright romantic to try and imagine that things-in-themselves can be thought without the human or that such a claim really means anything. It is questionable both on political grounds (the romanticism I just mentioned) and ontological ones, for it prefers to think from a potentiality rather than an actuality. For in actuality human beings do exist, and if one is going to engage with the world it is necessary to deal with the human. The drive to repress this actuality of the human in dealings with the world reveals something about the fundamental structure of the philosophical world – that for the World the human is not significant. That the concept of the All is more important than the things within. This is precisely a worldly logic as well, for the structure of the world is as an apparatus, a system, and it grinds upon the lived materiality of flesh and blood human (beings). The structure of the World, in its capitalist form and in its "naturalist" form (in the terms of philosophical naturalism), is simply Moloch – it grinds down on flesh and blood without concern for individuals. This vision of the World looks on without concern, and the claim these philosophers make is that, indeed, the world will churn on without any concern. But we know that there is concern in the world, however fleshy it may be, and it is still actual in human beings and likely in other creatures. Within a worldly vision there may be a debate between sentimentalists who will argue for the ultimate meaning behind this kind of concern and those who argue for a sort of absolute meaninglessness. But non-philosophy's vision refuses to be worldly: neither meaning nor meaninglessness is absolute; they are contingent, but the human, for all our contingency, still manifests, still persists in spite of the All, for the lived human is One-in-One without relation to the All.[34]

Let's end this short section by turning to Laruelle's remarks on speculative realism. When asked about his relationship to this nascent trend he replied:

> So, when I look at these movements (of Meillassoux, and so on), I do so with interest, with curiosity, but nothing more. With the pleasure that we have in seeing a showman who makes philosophy swing. I would respond with Marx's maxim: man is a natural being but he must make nature human. This is the redoubling of the man who is not a philosophical doublet. Man makes up part of nature, but it is by praxis that he makes nature human. This redoubling is also in another great formula of Marx: the fusion of productive forces and relations of production *under* the relations of production. This intensification is not the same kind as the philosophical doublet which is a redoubling of transcendence over itself, while, with Marx, it is a step toward an immanence; a simplification of transcendence. Meillassoux and the rest are very interesting but locked up within the philosophical decision.[35]

If the speculative turn is going to truly pass its own extensity test (or what we may call the non-extensity test) then it will need to break out of the philosophical decision that separates the political and the metaphysical, to in some sense transform the philosophical projection of nature and bring it under the condition of the Real which is the lived (experience) of the human victim.[36]

The refusal to absolutely separate the metaphysical and political realms points to something about non-philosophy that is very different from the return to metaphysics marked by speculative realism. Whereas speculative realism is a revival of philosophical faith, non-philosophy practices a kind of science of that faith, seeking to understand it and disempower it. The fact that non-philosophy aims to understand philosophy, to be a science of philosophy, would appear to align it with those extra-philosophical theorists like Bruno Latour or Pierre Bourdieu, who also refused to separate absolutely the metaphysical and political. Both these theorists have turned to disciplines outside philosophy in order to study philosophy itself; anthropology for Latour and sociology for Bourdieu, two disciplines that have historically undermined various forms of faith. Non-Philosophy, however, does not aim to be an empirical science surveying philosophy in this way and this is what differentiates Laruelle's project from those of Bourdieu and Latour. Non-Philosophy instead aims to trace the transcendental structures of philosophy (including those spontaneous philosophies present in sociology and anthropology) and the way in which it differentiates the transcendental and the empirical while ignoring the radical immanence of the One-in-One. This will require, then, a certain understanding of these two terms within non-philosophy that is very different from the standard philosophical form, which Laruelle traces out in his final chapter.

NON-PHILOSOPHY AND THE FECUNDITY OF TRANSLATION

The choice to write about Laruelle's relationship to speculative realism was largely arbitrary and was made mostly because in so far as speculative realism has become the common name for post-Continental philosophy it is important to see how Laruelle's non-philosophy finds no shelter there. Non-Philosophy is not suddenly at home with the resurgence of metaphysics regardless of their proclaimed materialist or realist bent. In a certain sense, non-philosophy is a kind of rigorous folk science, practiced by a kind of mad scientist who goes dumpster diving with a copy of Ginsburg's *Howl*. Non-Philosophy examines and uses the materials available to it, so one could take the method of non-philosophy and investigate the amphibologies inherent in Meillassoux or Harman and find some way to work them into various pragmatics of thought. But we could just as easily have picked up on the ways in which certain references are deployed without being made explicit. For those familiar with their philosophies may see aspects of Sartre, Heidegger, Husserl, Kant, Henry, Levinas, Derrida, Deleuze, Foucault, and others circulating at greater or lesser intensity throughout the final chapter of *Principles of Non-Philosophy*.

123

Certainly, none of these proper names nor any "reading" developed of them is the point for Laruelle, but the proliferation and conjugation of many different names is part of the non-philosophical project. In *Principles of Non-Philosophy* he sees this conjugation as a kind of translation between philosophies, one that is possible precisely because they are all equivalent as relative before the Real.

Thus, whether it is Kant or Marx or Descartes or whomever at play, it is a matter of translating them one into the other, of finding a way to speak in a tongue that is not one's own, to dwell in a territory one is a stranger to, and to be nowhere at home even as one may dwell anywhere.

> Non-philosophy *is* this translation of Kant 'into' Descartes, of Descartes 'into' Marx, of Marx 'into' Husserl, etc. That is to say under the condition of the vision-in-One as un-translatable Real. To put it more rigorously, no more than it is im-possible or un-symbolizable, the Real is not un-translatable, but is rather that which renders the possibility of translation real-in-the-last-instance, the Real itself being foreclosed, without negation, to any translation and not becoming the untranslatable other than as force-(of)-thought or, in this instance, *force-(of)-translation*. It is in this manner, through a translation of philosophical decisions or through solely transcendental equivalents of their respective identity, that a democracy that is not a simple transcendental appearance can be introduced into philosophy and between philosophies in place of their conflictual and hierarchical multiplicity.[37]

This fecund translatability within philosophies is what allows for the usual hierarchical practices of philosophy to be disempowered. As Laruelle remarks, "Even within thought, there is a democracy problem. And the conditions of democracy are those of an apparent minimalism linked to the radicality of immanence and the non-philosophical rigor of thought."[38]

This refusal of philosophical faith, of philosophical sufficiency, is also a refusal of the fantasy of the philosopher-king, just as much as it is a refusal of the figure of the pseudo-democracy found in representative democratic societies. This is a democracy without representation, an un-presentable democracy, a utopia. And, to transpose the philosophical into the political realm, this is what marks the ultimate difference between the two figures who tower over the final chapter of *Principles of Non-Philosophy*: Kant and Husserl. Both perform a Philosophical Decision between the empirical and the transcendental, Kant cleaving the appearance of a thing and the thing-in-itself, with Husserl breaking the noesis and noema or the "I-pole" and "object-pole" of perception (itself a kind of phenomenological restruc-turing of the phenomenal/noumenal split in Kant).[39] While both Kant and Husserl claim to speak about reality as such through these decisions, Laruelle relativizes the claims produced by their decisions and considers them in relation to philosophy alone. So he asks about experience and the transcendental, but in relation to philosophy alone, rather than as a universal and determining aspect of reality or human perception.[40]

Kant's philosophy marks a kind of pseudo-democracy in thought, famously limiting knowledge to make room for faith while also setting reason as a kind of tribunal that would fall into neither nomadic hatred for civil society nor into a kind of absolute monarchism within thought.[41] To do this Kant needed to show the limits of pure reason, that is, what may be known prior to experience, and to do that he needed to know how synthetic a priori judgments were possible. Such judgments are not derived directly from their objects and yet produce new knowledge outside of experience. The newness of that knowledge is what appears important for Laruelle when he writes: "We abandon the question: 'how are synthetic a priori judgments possible?' for this one: 'what can we discover of the new, the non-synthetic, with the help of synthetic a priori judgments, i.e. with philosophy?' This is the whole problem for non-philosophy, if we can summarize it and present it with Kantian material."[42]

There is a kind of philosopher-messiah fatigue amongst readers of (post-)Continental philosophy. When a philosopher who is unfamiliar to Anglophone readers begins to be translated, grandiose claims are often made about the importance of their work, about the possibilities inherent in studying them, or even of the unique ways in which they may change our social and political actions or at least our relation to them. Laruelle is no messiah. Or, to be more accurate and following the line he takes on the question of messianism, he is no more a messiah than any other Human-in-person. The point of studying non-philosophy, of taking the time to read Laruelle and texts like this one that claim to aid in that task, is not to enthrone yet another philosopher-king or to replace the fallen French kings of philosophy. Let us be done with kings, let us be done with pseudo-democrats, and let us be done with the industries produced around them. Let there be no "Laruelle studies," but instead let there be a proliferation of non-philosophical projects. Texts like this one are perhaps necessary, if only as another product of the fecundity of translation (and fecundity also involves a lot of failure, lest someone think that as a translator I am making any special claims to unique knowledge). Yet, non-philosophy would be a failure if only texts like this were produced. Thankfully, in the Anglophone literature on Laruelle, we have seen creative works that take up the non-philosophical method instead of the standard model of philosophical exegesis. For Laruelle helps us to find a certain rigor of thought alongside of a wild freedom to think and requires no oaths of fealty nor genuflection. My hope is that this introduction and guide has helped the reader to understand some of the more fecund concepts and aspects of the non-philosophical method so that new non-philosophical works may bloom. These works will manifest a certain frailty as well as power, a certain sense of what it means to One-in-One. That is, a certain sense of what it means to be a creature, a human being, nowhere at home and yet able to speak in a multitude of strange tongues.

Notes

INTRODUCTION

1. For a short piece by Laruelle exploring the theme of communicability
   see his "The Truth According to Hermes: Theorems on the Secret and
   Communication," trans. Alexander R. Galloway, in *Parrhesia* 9 (2010): 18–22.
   See also Alexander R. Galloway, Eugene Thacker, and McKenzie Wark,
   Excommunication: Three Inquiries in Media and Mediation (Chicago: Chicago
   University Press, 2014) for various uses of Laruelle to address the theme of
   communicability and media.
2. Readers interested in various readings of Laruelle that have been taken
   up by other Anglophone philosophers and theorists may find of interest
   Anthony Paul Smith, *A Non-Philosophical Theory of Nature: Ecologies of
   Thought* (New York and London: Palgrave Macmillan, 2013), Katerina
   Kolozova, *Cut of the Real: Subjectivity in Poststructuralist* Philosophy (New
   York: Columbia University Press, 2014), John Ó Maoilearca, *All Thoughts
   Are Equal: Laruelle and Nonhuman Philosophy* (Minneapolis: University
   of Minnesota Press, 2015), and Alexander R. Galloway, *Laruelle: Against
   the Digital*, (Minneapolis: University of Minnesota Press, 2014), alongside of the already established readings by Ray Brassier, *Nihil Unbound:
   Enlightenment and Extinction* (Basingstoke: Palgrave, 2007), Chapter 5, and
   Ian James, *The New French Philosophy* (Cambridge: Polity, 2012), Chapter
   7, which promises a forthcoming book that engages with Laruelle in a
   central way to examine questions of technique and the experimental nature
   of contemporary philosophy.
3. Brassier and Ó Maoilearca use these two terms to describe non-philosophical
   practice.
4. When referring to Laruelle's mutation of the concept of "determination
   in the last instance" I follow his grapheme which places hyphens between
   each word and when I discuss the Marxist conception I write it without the
   hyphens.
5. See Smith, *A Non-Philosophical Theory of Nature*, pp. 73–81.

CHAPTER 1

1. Readers should consult Rocco Gangle, *François Laruelle's* Philosophies of Difference: *A Critical Introduction and Guide* (Edinburgh: Edinburgh University Press, 2013), for a clear explication of this earlier work.
2. PNP, p. 13.
3. Readers who wish to see what this non-philosophical vision of transdisciplinary work can look like should consult the work of Anne-Françoise Schmid. In particular, they may wish to consult "The Science-Thought of Laruelle and its Effects on Epistemology" in *Laruelle and Non-Philosophy*, ed. John Ó Maoilearca and Anthony Paul Smith (Edinburgh: Edinburgh University Press, 2012), pp. 122–42, and Anne-Françoise Schmid and Armand Hatchuel, "On Generic Epistemology," *Angelaki: Journal of the Theoretical Humanities* 19.2 (2014): 131–44. Readers may also wish to consult my own interdisciplinary work, *A Non-Philosophical Theory of Nature*, where I use the methodology of non-philosophy to bring together philosophical theology and scientific ecology.
4. This intense exploration of the identity of the human or "Man" begins in one of his earliest non-philosophical texts, *Une Biographie de l'homme ordinaire. Des Autorités et des Minorités* (Paris: Aubier, 1985), and continues in his mature works like *Future Christ: A Lesson in Heresy*, trans. Anthony Paul Smith (London and New York: Continuum, 2010) and *Struggle and Utopia at the End Times of Philosophy*, trans. Drew S. Burk and Anthony Paul Smith (Minneapolis: Univocal Publishing, 2012).
5. In recent work he has given attention to the status of the "victim" and this has opened his analysis up to the consideration of non-human subjects. See *General Theory of Victims*, trans. Jessie Hock and Alex Dubilet (Cambridge: Polity, 2015), pp. 102–5. Readers interested in what Laruelle's non-philosophy may have to offer to our understanding of animals should consult John Ó Maoilearca, "The Animal Line: On the Possibility of a 'Laruellean' Non-Human Philosophy," *Angelaki: Journal of the Theoretical Humanities* 19.2 (2014): 113–29, and Ó Maoilearca, *All Thoughts Are Equal: Laruelle and Nonhuman Philosophy*.
6. For this history of non-philosophy focusing on its changes in terms of axioms, see Smith, *A Non-Philosophical Theory of Nature*, pp. 73–81, and Gangle, *François Laruelle's* Philosophies of Difference, pp. 15–20, for a more sustained analysis of this periodization as well as more details on each phase.
7. PNP, p. 2.
8. PNP, p. 2.
9. PNP, p. 13.
10. François Laruelle, "Non-Philosophy, Weapon of Last Defence" in *Laruelle and Non-Philosophy*, ed. Ó Maoilearca and Smith, p. 239.
11. PNP, p. xxi.
12. While the theory of the Philosophical Decision is extremely important to Laruelle's work, I will not be discussing it at length here. The reason for

this is that Philosophical Decision was the focal point of Laruelle's original Anglophone reception and while it was often erroneously conflated with Meillassoux's critique of correlationism, there nonetheless already exist a number of useful introductory discussions of the notion. See Brassier, *Nihil Unbound*, pp. 120–7, for a highly technical discussion, and John Ó Maoilearca, *Post-Continental Philosophy: An Outline* (London and New York: Routledge, 2006), pp. 140–4, for a more accessible discussion, but also Laruelle's own discussion in PD, pp. 196–223, and Gangle, *François Laruelle's* Philosophies of Difference, pp. 153–4, 164–71.

13. PNP, p. 13.
14. PNP, p. 20.
15. PNP, p. 17.
16. PNP, p. 22
17. Gilles Deleuze and Félix Guattari, *What Is Philosophy?*, trans. Hugh Tomlinson and Graham Burchell (New York: Columbia University Press, 1994), pp. 44–9.
18. SU, pp. 176, 177–9.
19. Readers interested in this aspect of Henry's theological work and its relationship to technology should consult Michel Henry, *I Am the Truth: Toward a Philosophy of Christianity*, trans. Susan Emanuel (Stanford: Stanford University Press, 2003), especially his remarks on Galileo, pp. 36, 72, 259–61, and Michel Henry, *Words of Christ*, trans. Christina M. Gschwandtner (Grand Rapids: William B. Eerdmans Publishing Co., 2012), as well as Christina M. Gschwandtner, *Postmodern Apologetics?: Arguments for God in Contemporary Philosophy* (New York: Fordham University Press, 2013), pp. 125–42, for a sympathetic reading of Henry as an orthodox Catholic philosopher-theologian. For his more general criticism of contemporary techno-culture see Michel Henry, *Barbarism*, trans. Scott Davidson (London and New York: Continuum, 2012), and Michel Henry, *From Communism to Capitalism: Theory of a Catastrophe*, trans. Scott Davidson (London and New York: Bloomsbury, 2014). For his reading of Marx see Michel Henry, *Marx: A Philosophy of Human Being*, trans. K. McLaughlin (Bloomington: Indiana University Press, 1983), which is an abridged translation of the original two-volume work in French.
20. Michel Henry, *The Essence of Manifestation*, trans. Girard Etzkorn (The Hague: Martinus Nijhoff, 1973), p. 96.
21. Ibid., p. 77.
22. Ibid., p. 62.
23. Ibid., p. 70.
24. See ibid., pp. 135–278.
25. Ibid., p. 130.
26. Ibid., p. 281.
27. Ibid., pp. 273–5.
28. See NM, pp. 43–6.
29. PNP, p. 18.

CHAPTER 2

1. See Alain Badiou *Being and Event*, trans. Oliver Feltham (London and New York: Continuum, 2005), especially his "Introduction" and Part I of the book.
2. See Martin Heidegger, *What Is Called Thinking?*, trans. J. Glenn Grey (New York: Harper & Row, 1968), p. 8 and the rest of the lecture. For a more tightly organized and historical discussion by Heidegger concerning how he understands the relationship between philosophy and the sciences, see Martin Heidegger, "Modern Science, Metaphysics, and Mathematics" in *Basic Writings*, ed. and trans. David Farrell Krell (New York: HarperSanFrancisco, 1993), pp. 267–305.
3. Laruelle's use of the French word *posture* has been translated by other translators of his work as "stance," whereas I and some others have translated it as "posture." I prefer "posture" because as a concept it is more immanent in Laruelle's sense, relating to the way the body holds itself, whereas I understand stance to be more of a relative term where it is about the relation of that body to some other body or within some other space. However, the quibbles of translators are potentially infinite and often distracting for the reader of the text. Each translator has their own good reasons for the choices they make and rarely are these choices made easily. So it is only important that the reader understand that when they read either "posture" or "stance" in a text by Laruelle or on Laruelle it is relating to the same word. In this text I will continue to use posture.
4. PNP, p. xviii.
5. PNP, p. 47.
6. See PNP, pp. 48–9.
7. See PNP, p. 40, for this exact definition of philosophy.
8. This point appears to share much in common with Adorno's concept of "non-identity," which is Adorno's own attempt to navigate the relationship of identity and difference. A fruitful research project would be a comparative study of Adorno and Laruelle's respective projects that we may traditionally call "philosophy of science."
9. PNP, p. 50.
10. Edmund Husserl, *Ideas I: General Introduction to Pure Phenomenology*, trans. W. R. Boyce Gibson (London and New York: Routledge, 2012), p. 219.
11. Dan Zahavi, *Husserl's Phenomenology* (Stanford: Stanford University Press, 2003), p. 39.
12. Husserl, *Ideas*, p. 146.
13. PNP, p. 63.
14. PNP, p. 66.
15. For more on difference and Laruelle's development of this concept see his PD and Gangle, *François Laruelle's* Philosophies of Difference.
16. PNP, p. 65.
17. Much of our discussion of Gödel's theorems and its relation to earlier works, like those of Hilbert, Russell and Whitehead, is dependent upon Ernest Nagel

and James R. Newman's popular *Gödel's Proof* (London and New York: New York University Press, 2001). This was originally published in 1958 and published in a revised edition in 2001 edited by Douglas R. Hofstadter. In addition to *Gödel's Proof*, readers interested in a relatively nontechnical explication of Gödel's theorem and its effects on logic and mathematics and related practical fields should consult Douglas R. Hofstadter's *Gödel, Escher, Bach: An Eternal Golden Braid* (New York: Basic Books, 1979) and his more recent *I Am a Strange Loop* (New York: Basic Books, 2007).

18. Nagel and Newman, *Gödel's Proof*, pp. 4–6.
19. Ibid., p. 58.
20. See Kurt Gödel, *On Formally Undecidable Propositions of* Principia Mathematica *and Related Systems*, trans. B. Meltzer (New York: Dover Publications, Inc., 1992), pp. 70–2.
21. The Figure is from Nagel and Newman. See *Gödel's Proof*, pp. 68–80, for more explanation of Gödel numbers.
22. Ibid., pp. 92–3.
23. Ibid., p. 104.
24. The preceding discussion of Gödel is largely derived from ibid., pp. 92–108.
25. PNP, p. 68.
26. PNP, p. 76.
27. PNP, p. 69.
28. PNP, p. 73.
29. PNP, p. 69.

CHAPTER 3

1. Gangle, *François Laruelle's* Philosophies of Difference, p. 18.
2. PNP, p. 84.
3. PNP, pp. 79–80.
4. PNP, p. 80.
5. The best resource for readers interested in this aspect of French thought, which has been neglected by Anglophone readers until very recently, is the *Cahiers pour l'Analyse* volumes recently edited and translated into English. See Peter Hallward and Knox Peden (eds), *Concept and Form, Volume 1: Key Texts from the* Cahiers pour l'Analyse (London: Verso, 2012). The group around the journal focused on structural epistemological questions, tending towards formalism in their expression, in psychoanalysis. For a polemical history of this period see Knox Peden, *Spinoza contra Phenomenology: French Rationalism from Cavaillès to Deleuze* (Stanford: Stanford University Press, 2014), and for a more evenhanded approach see Tom Eyers, *Post-Rationalism: Psychoanalysis, Epistemology, and Marxism in Post-War France* (London: Bloomsbury, 2013).
6. PNP, p. 80.
7. PNP, p. 90.
8. Olivier Boulnois, "Object" in *Dictionary of Untranslatables: A Philosophical*

Lexicon, ed. Barbara Cassin, trans. Steven Rendall, Christian Hubert, Jeffrey Mehlman, Nathanael Stein, and Michael Syrotinski (Princeton: Princeton University Press, 2014), p. 724.

9. Ibid. Boulnois' summary of the transition from a medieval to a modern epistemological conception of the object is interesting for students of Laruelle's non-philosophy for its central metaphor of vision: "What is known is no longer the face of the thing itself, but the obstacle with which the look collides, that deprives its activity of its own transparency. Knowledge is no longer a simple reception of an actual being by the power moved, but rather the ricochet of a ray emitted by the intellect that is reflected back to it after having bounced off its terminus" (p. 725).

10. See Immanuel Kant, *Critique of Pure Reason*, trans. Paul Guyer and Allen W. Wood (Cambridge: Cambridge University Press, 1998), §16, B132. For a truncated but insightful summary of the way the subject is cast in Kant, see Étienne Balibar, Barbara Cassin, and Alain de Libera, "Subject" in *Dictionary of Untranslatables: A Philosophical Lexicon*, ed. Barbara Cassin, trans. David Macey, pp. 1080–3.

11. Again, readers should consult Ó Maoilearca, Brassier, and Gangle respectively on the philosophical decision. See footnote 12 in Chapter 1 above.

12. Marion's oeuvre is vast, but readers looking to engage with works of importance to Laruelle should consult Marion's influential *God Without Being: Hors-Texte*, 2nd edition, trans. Thomas A. Carlson (Chicago: University of Chicago Press, 2012), which has had an influence on Laruelle's thinking regarding religion as evidenced by the presence of "God-without-Being" in DNP, pp. 73–4. Of his important works on the foundational and methodological aspects of phenomenology, influential upon Laruelle's understanding of givenness and conception of the given-without-givenness, are *Reduction and Givenness: Investigations of Husserl, Heidegger, and Phenomenology*, trans. Thomas A. Carlson (Chicago: Northwestern University Press, 1998) and *Being Given: Toward a Phenomenology of Givenness*, trans. Jeffery Kosky (Stanford: Stanford University Press, 2002). Marion has published a trilogy of historical studies on Cartesian philosophy, in addition to editing Descartes' *Regulae ad directionem ingenii* (*Rules for the Direction of the Mind*), a text that he explores in Jean-Luc Marion, *Descartes' Grey Ontology: Cartesian Science and Aristotelian Thought in the* Regulae, trans. Sarah Donahue (South Bend, IN: St. Augustine's Press, 2014), originally published in French in 1975, followed by Jean-Luc Marion, *Sur la théologie blanche de Descartes. Analogie, création des vérités éternelles, fondement* (Paris: PUF, 1981), and most importantly for Laruelle's construction of the history in *Principles of Non-Philosophy*, Jean-Luc Marion, *On Descartes' Metaphysical Prism: The Constitution and Limits of Onto-theo-logy in Cartesian Thought*, trans. Jeffrey L. Kosky (Chicago: Chicago University Press, 1999), originally published in 1986.

13. Marion, *On Descartes' Metaphysical Prism*, p. 150.

14. Ibid., pp. 143–4.

15. PNP, p. 97.

16. PNP, pp. 97–8.
17. PNP, p. 97.
18. PNP, pp. 96–7.
19. PNP, p. 106.
20. PNP, pp. 105–6 (my emphasis).
21. PNP, p. 107.
22. Henry, *I Am the Truth*, p. 34.
23. Ibid., p. 105 (translation slightly modified).
24. PNP, p. 115.
25. Henry, *I Am the Truth*, p. 105 (my emphasis).
26. Henry's own anti-scientism is far more radical than Husserl's criticism of the sciences in relation to what he terms the "life-world." Husserl sought to correct the sciences through a grounding in transcendental phenomenology, while Henry appears to see the sciences, especially as techno-capitalist science, as a near absolute threat to human dignity. See Henry, *Barbarism*, and Edmund Husserl, *The Crisis of European Sciences and Transcendental Phenomenology: An Introduction to Phenomenological Philosophy*, trans. David Carr (Chicago: Northwestern University Press, 1970), especially §9 for the influence on Henry and §34 for the possibility of a phenomenological correction to the sciences.
27. PNP, p. 111.
28. PNP, p. 106.

CHAPTER 4

1. Laruelle, "Non-Philosophy, Weapon of Last Defence," p. 247.
2. PNP, p. 158.
3. Daniel Breazeale, "Fichte's Conception of Philosophy as a 'Pragmatic History of the Human Mind' and the Contributions of Kant, Platner, and Maimon," *Journal of the History of Ideas* 62.4 (2001): 692.
4. Immanuel Kant, *Werke. Akademie-Textausgabe* VII (Berlin, 1968), p. 119, quoted in Breazeale, "Fichte's Conception of Philosophy," p. 688.
5. PNP, p. 122.
6. PNP, p. 121.
7. PNP, p. 121.
8. For the most extended treatment of the quantum see PNS. For a shorter example in English translation of the way in which Laruelle's engagement with quantum physics shapes his rethinking of standard philosophical categories like ethics, see François Laruelle "Principles for a Generic Ethics," trans. Anthony Paul Smith, *Angelaki: Journal of the Theoretical Humanities* 19.2 (2014): 12–23.
9. For an overview of the concept of the One as it relates both to standard philosophy and Laruelle's recasting of it, see Anthony Paul Smith, "Thinking from the One: Non-Philosophy and the Ancient Philosophical Figure of the One" in *Laruelle and Non-Philosophy*, ed. Ó Maoilearca and Smith, pp. 19–41.

10. See Emmanuel Levinas, *Otherwise than Being: Or Beyond Essence*, trans. Alphonso Lingis (Pittsburgh: Duquesne University Press, 1998). There Levinas writes, "Transcendence is passing over to being's *other*, otherwise than being. Not *to be otherwise*, but *otherwise than being*. And not to not-be; passing over is not here equivalent to dying. Being and not-being illuminate one another, and unfold a speculative dialectic which is a determination of being. Or else the negativity which attempts to repel being is immediately filled with the mute and anonymous rustling of the there is [*il y a*], as the place left vacant by one who died is filled with the murmur of the attendants" (p. 3). The rest of the book is devoted to describing the encounter with the Other as this form of transcendence which structures the very thinking of Being. This builds on Emmanuel Levinas, *Totality and Infinity: An Essay on Exteriority*, trans. Alphonso Lingis (Pittsburgh: Duquesne University Press, 1969). There he writes, "critique does not reduce the other to the same as does ontology, but calls into question the exercise of the same. A calling into question of the same – which cannot occur within the egoist spontaneity of the same – is brought about by the other. We name this calling into question of my spontaneity by the presence of the Other ethics. The strangeness of the Other, his irreducibility to the I, to my thoughts and my possessions, is precisely accomplished as a calling into question of my spontaneity, as ethics. Metaphysics, transcendence, the welcoming of the other by the same, of the Other by me, is concretely produced as the calling into question of the same by the other, that is, as the ethics that accomplishes the critical essence of knowledge. And as critique precedes dogmatism, metaphysics precedes ontology. [...] If ontology – the comprehension, the embracing of Being – is impossible, it is not because every definition of Being already presupposes the knowledge of Being, as Pascal had said and Heidegger refutes in the first pages of *Being and Time*; it is because the comprehension of Being in general cannot dominate the relationship with the Other. The latter relationship commands the first. I cannot disentangle myself from society with the Other, even when I consider the Being of the existent he is" (pp. 43, 47).

11. In the next chapter we address Laruelle's casting of the terms "Greek" and "Jew" throughout his corpus, especially when writing about Derrida or Levinas, but see also Anthony Paul Smith, "François Laruelle" in *Religion and European Philosophy: Key Thinkers from Kant to Today*, ed. Philip Goodchild and Hollis D. Phelps (New York and London: Routledge, Forthcoming). This includes a further response to the misunderstandings present in certain attempts to criticize Laruelle's use of the term "Judaic" as anti-Semitic.

12. PNP, p. 122.

13. PNP, pp. 125–6.

14. PNP, p. 126.

15. Daniel W. Smith, "The Doctrine of Univocity: Deleuze's Ontology of Immanence" in *Deleuze and Religion*, ed. Mary Bryden (London and New York: Routledge, 2001), p. 173.

16. See PNP, p. 126 specifically, but pp. 125–9 for his own expanded and clear exposition of this difference.
17. NM, p. 42.
18. See PNP, p. 122.
19. PNP, p. 124.
20. PNP, p. 128.
21. "But we know through the philosophers themselves, in an undoubtedly still limited manner, that they do not say what they are doing, and do not do what they are saying. In particular, they neither exclude nor destroy metaphysics as they say they do, nor do they access the Real when they claim to" (PNP, p. 142).
22. PNP, p. 146.
23. PNP, p. 140.
24. PNP, p. 144.
25. PNP, p. 147.
26. PNP, p. 140.
27. J. G. Fichte, *Science of Knowledge*, trans. and ed. Peter Heath and John Lachs (Cambridge: Cambridge University Press, 1982), p. 6.
28. See François Laruelle and Anne-Françoise Schmid, "Sexed Identity," trans. Nicola Rubczak, *Angelaki: Journal of the Theoretical Humanities* 19.2 (2014): 35–9.
29. Fichte, *Science of Knowledge*, p. 6.
30. See Laruelle, "Non-Philosophy, Weapon of Last Defence," p. 241, and François Laruelle, "A Rigorous Science of Man" in *From Decision to Heresy: Experiments in Non-Standard Thought*, trans. and ed. Robin Mackay (Falmouth: Urbanomic, 2012), pp. 39–40.
31. PNP, pp. 158, 140.
32. Frederick Neuhouser, *Fichte's Theory of Subjectivity* (Cambridge: Cambridge University Press, 1990), p. 6.
33. Fichte, *Science of Knowledge*, p. 54.
34. For Fichte's own summary of this principle see ibid., pp. 93–102.
35. For an explication more focused on Kant and Fichte see Michael Kolkman, "Kant and Fichte on Intellectual Intuition" (Unpublished paper, 2010), available online at <https://www.academia.edu/2576743/Kant_and_Fichte_on_Intellectual_Intuition> (last accessed November 23, 2014).
36. See Kant, *Critique of Pure Reason*, §10.
37. Neuhouser, *Fichte's Theory of Subjectivity*, p. 77.
38. "The I think must be able to accompany all my representations, for otherwise something would be represented in me that could not be thought at all, which is as much as to say that the representation would either be impossible or else at least would be nothing for me. That representation that can be given prior to all thinking is called intuition" (Kant, *Critique of Pure Reason*, B132).
39. PNP, p. 140. This is the stated reason for Ray Brassier's use of Laruelle in *Nihil Unbound* as a way to radicalize certain philosophical moves in Meillassoux's *After Finitude* (Brassier, *Nihil Unbound*, p. 139). This is worth noting because

while Brassier has in public lectures expressed a certain moving away from his work in *Nihil Unbound*, it still remains an important text for students attracted to non-philosophy as a method. Compare also the presentations and discussion between Meillassoux and Brassier at the 2007 "Speculative Realism" event, transcribed and published in *Collapse* (Ray Brassier, Iain Hamilton Grant, Graham Harman, and Quentin Meillassoux, "Speculative Realism," in *Collapse III* (Falmouth: Urbanomic, 2007), pp. 307–449).

40. See TI, p. 56.
41. See PNS, p. 54.
42. See Fichte, *Science of Knowledge*, pp. 102–5, for his summary of this principle.
43. Ibid., p. 105.
44. PNP, p. 144
45. PNP, p. 146.
46. PNP, p. 145.
47. For Fichte's summary of the third principle see Fichte, *Science of Knowledge*, pp. 105–19. Owing to the complexity of this principle, since it references the other two, this summary is considerably longer and reads almost as if it were a theorem in Laruelle's sense rather than a simple principle.
48. Ibid., p. 110.
49. It is worth mentioning that this notion of I = I is called a thetic judgment by Fichte and this notion of thetic transcendence is taken up by Laruelle, especially in PD (pp. 202–3). See my use of this schema in Smith, *A Non-Philosophical Theory of Nature*, pp. 220–2, for an example of how it may be used. See also Alexander R. Galloway's own exploration of Laruelle's relation to Fichte contra Kant on reason in "The Autism of Reason," *Angelaki: Journal of the Theoretical Humanities* 19.2 (2014): 73–83.
50. Fichte, *Science of Knowledge*, pp. 110–11.
51. PNP, p. 147.
52. Laruelle gets at this somewhat obliquely when he writes:

> Let us return to the problem of duality. If duality is called unilateral because it is only thinkable from the (second) term – the non(-One), it is also and more profoundly unilateralized through an effect of the (non-) One which comes under the same transcendental status as unidentity. Just as the relation or transcendence is affected by a transcendental identity, it is affected by a transcendental unilaterality, from a real though conditional origin that is consequently dependent on a "subject" which is affected by it. We do not immediately confuse unilateral duality in the first sense and the unilateralization or the (non-)One which affects it as clone of the One and which precisely finds a subject or a support in the first. Transcendental unilateralization can equally be said to form a unilateral duality or more precisely a *duality of unilateralization* between transcendental unidentity and the empirical term which, in this instance, is a relation or transcendence itself. In reality these two unilateral dualities come back to themselves by forming one structure, first glimpsed

from the transcendental term and secondly from its empirical cause. If for example transcendence presents itself, it must in any case be lived-in-One and, consequently, identified/reduced by the Real but specifically in a transcendental manner. Unilateralization is thus a radical form of transcendental reduction but it does not occur without transcendental identity. (PNP, pp. 132–3)

We see here that ultimately the (non-)One is a name for the radical or more general unilateralization that occurs at local levels in philosophical doublets.

53. PNP, p. 144.
54. Graham Harman, "Review of François Laruelle's *Philosophies of Difference: A Critical Introduction to Non-Philosophy*," *Notre Dame Philosophical Reviews* (12 August 2011), available online at <https://ndpr.nd.edu/news/25437-philosophies-of-difference-a-critical-introduction-to-non-philosophy> (last accessed May 27, 2015).
55. PD, p. 179.
56. PNP, p. 148.
57. There he writes, "Force-(of)-thought is a complex concept. The One cannot act of itself, for only Being or Transcendence can act upon philosophical material, i.e. a universal exteriority that functions as an organon for the One. [...] In effect, Being is the *a priori* which structures every theory produced by thought and which as such is itself presupposed in its existence, but the transcendental Identity that precedes it and makes a transcendental subject of the force-(of)-thought radically halts this circularity because the force-(of)-thought is a clone entirely produced 'under' One or 'according to' the One" (DNP, pp. 64–5 (translation slightly modified)). Prior to this linking of the force-(of)-thought to the clone we find his succinct definition of the force-(of)-thought: "Organon or the means through which the One can enact or possess a causality without being alienated in the material of its action. Instance which is not real like the One but produced by cloning. Transcendental and aprioristic, it has its real essence in the One without adding anything to or subtracting anything from the Real itself, which determines it in-the-last-instance relative to an occasion" (DNP, p. 63).
58. Cf. IP, pp. 49–50.
59. PNP, p. 138.
60. IP, pp. 50, 51. This text is the edited transcript of a conversation with Philippe Petit and published under the French title *L'Ultime honneur des intellectuels*.

CHAPTER 5

1. PNP, p. 187.
2. PNP, p. 202.
3. Ibid.
4. PNP, p. 302.
5. Andrew McGettigan, "Fabrication Defect: François Laruelle's Philosophical Materials," *Radical Philosophy* 175 (September/October 2012), pp. 33–42.

6. One of the few edited volumes that Laruelle oversaw without a focus upon his own project of non-philosophy was *Textes Pour Emmanuel Lévinas* (Paris: Editions Jean-Michel Place, 1980). As well as an essay by Laruelle, this volume brought together major French philosophers and other intellectuals like Maurice Blanchot, Jean-François Lyotard, Paul Ricoeur, Edmond Jabès, amongst others. It serves in itself to counter Andrew McGettigan's irresponsible claim that Levinas is "another Jew but not a philosopher for Laruelle" (McGettigan, "Fabrication Defect," p. 35).

7. Laruelle's early work was all devoted to political concerns. Much of it prefigured work that is popular in left-wing theoretical circles today, with discussions of the "multitude" and a kind of political dualism between "minorities" and "authorities" that echoes Antonio Negri's distinction between constitutive and constituted power, though cast more explicitly as a unilateral duality that arguably can be read in Negri's text as well. Furthermore, in an earlier text, "minorities" are cast as the principle by which to think mereology or the relationship of part to a whole. See François Laruelle, *Nietzsche contra Heidegger. Thèses pour une politique nietzschéene* (Paris: Payot, 1977) on multitude. See François Laruelle, *Une Biographie de l'homme ordinaire. Des Autorités et des Minorités* (Paris: Aubier, 1985) for the dualysis of the political dualism between minorities and authorities. See François Laruelle, *Le Principe de minorité* (Paris: Aubier, 1981) for his conjugation of politics and mereology. Much of the criticism in McGettigan's article reveals his own lack of research into Laruelle's work, a lack of scholarly focus he ironically bemoans early in the article (McGettigan, "Fabrication Defect," p. 33).

8. Laruelle quoted in Robin Mackay, "Introduction: Laruelle Undivided" in *From Decision to Heresy: Experiments in Non-Standard Thought*, pp. 11–12.

9. Ultimately even McGettigan implies what he denies, when he claims these are descriptions of deconstruction and not Derrida the subject (McGettigan, "Fabrication Defect," p. 37).

10. See Gangle, *François Laruelle's* Philosophies of Difference, pp. 136–7 for explication of Laruelle's reading of Derrida's double-band.

11. McGettigan, "Fabrication Defect," p. 37.

12. As paradigmatic of Derrida's ability to struggle and produce from that struggle, the reader should consult the beautiful "Circumfession" in *Jacques Derrida*, trans. Geoffrey Bennington (Chicago: University of Chicago, 1999). One wonders if McGettigan would object to Derrida's close friend and colleague Hélène Cixous describing Derrida as a Jew, which she developed over the course of an entire book: *Portrait of Jacques Derrida as a Young Jewish Saint*, trans. Beverley Bie Brahic (New York: Columbia University Press, 2004). For her own discussion of Derrida as a *marrano*, a term that appears to greatly offend McGettigan perhaps owing to a lack of understanding of the Jewish religion and the history of positive reclamation of the term by Jewish intellectuals, see Cixious, *Portrait*, pp. 113–14. On Derrida's own discussion of the way in which Levinas "feigned to speak Greek in order to get near the king" with the purpose of killing him, see Jacques Derrida, "Violence and

Metaphysics: An Essay on the Thought of Emmanuel Levinas" in *Writing and Difference*, trans. Alan Bass (London and New York: Routledge, 2001), p. 110.

13. PNP, p. 169.
14. Derrida, "Violence and Metaphysics," p. 192.
15. Ibid., p. 100.
16. Ibid., p. 190.
17. Ibid., p. 119. Cf. p. 100.
18. Ibid., p. 190.
19. PNP, pp. 170–1.
20. Derrida, "Violence and Metaphysics," pp. 191–2.
21. EU, p. 235.
22. "On the other hand, a thought of the One signifies that this struggle is no longer our business. We are no longer interested, even if analysts would like us each to carry our 'Torah' in lieu and in place of Greek destiny. The appeal to the joint authorities of Parmenides and the Bible, Plato and the Talmud, cannot convince a spirit which places itself under the law of 'phenomena' alone" (PNP, p. 169).
23. PNP, p. 174.
24. PNP, p. 186.
25. PNP, p. 178.
26. For a more extended version of this argument and fuller exploration of Laruelle's conception of the human in dialogue with critical race theory see my *Laruelle: A Stranger Thought*.
27. Deleuze and Guattari, *What Is Philosophy?*, p. 43.
28. PNP, p. 209.
29. PNP, p. 203.
30. PNP, pp. 204–5.
31. Max Horkheimer and Theodor W. Adorno, *Dialectic of Enlightenment: Philosophical Fragments*, ed. Gunzelin Schmid Noerr, trans. Edmund Jephcott (Stanford: Stanford University Press, 2002), p. 22.
32. Ibid., p. 35.
33. PNP, p. 205.
34. Horkheimer and Adorno, *Dialectic of Enlightenment*, p. 172.
35. PNP p. 205.
36. See Catherine Bell, *Ritual Theory, Ritual Practice* (Oxford: Oxford University Press, 2009). Bell engages with anthropologists but also with important French philosophical voices like Réne Girard and Michel Foucault.
37. PNP, p. 208.
38. PNP, p. 208.
39. PNP, p. 206.
40. PNP, p. 207.
41. PNP, pp. 207–8.
42. PNP, p. 212.
43. PNP, p. 212.
44. PNP, p. 265. Readers interested in Laruelle's "real critique of reason" should also consult pp. 263–5.

45. PNP, p. 222.
46. Alain Badiou, *The Century*, trans. Alberto Toscano (Cambridge: Polity, 2007), pp. 215, fn. 51. The disdain is made explicit in a recent interview. See Alain Badiou, "Interview with Ben Woodard" in *The Speculative Turn: Continental Materialism and Realism*, ed. Levi Bryant, Nick Srnicek, and Graham Harman (Melbourne: re:press, 2011), p. 20.
47. Badiou, *The Century*, pp. 54–6.
48. PNP, p. 217.
49. PNP, p. 221.
50. PNP, p. 221.
51. PNP, p. 221.
52. PNP, p. 221.
53. Henry, *I Am the Truth*, pp. 25, 38. Henry is quoting the French biologist François Jacob from his *The Logic of Life*. Jacob was an important figure for other French philosophers as well, most notably Deleuze.
54. PNP, p. 222.
55. Brassier, *Nihil Unbound*, pp. 238–9.
56. He very explicitly writes in the introduction to his chapter on Laruelle, "Thus we will try to show why Laruelle's non-philosophy is not just a curious but ultimately bootless exercise in extravagant sterility by arguing – against Laruelle himself – that its conceptual import can and should be philosophically interpreted" (ibid., pp. 119–20).
57. I have referred to these as Kantian and post-Kantian as this is the common practice in Anglophone philosophy. Laruelle, however, might refer to them as "Cartesian and post-Cartesian philosophies," which would encompass Kant's critical project as well. This is a common practice in French philosophy, as evidenced by chapter 3 of *Principles of Non-Philosophy*, as well as Marion's work cited in this guide. What remains important is not the proper name deployed, but the emphasis on the relation between subject and object, or reason and experience, that is assumed operative in these philosophies.
58. See Michel Foucault, *The Order of Things: An Archeology of the Human Sciences* (London: Routledge, 2002), p. 172: "all [inquiries of a philosophical and scientific nature] rested upon a sort of historical *a priori*, which authorized them in their dispersion and in their singular and divergent projects, and rendered equally possible all the differences of opinion of which they were the source. This *a priori* does not consist of a set of constant problems uninterruptedly presented to men's curiosity by concrete phenomena as so many enigmas; nor is it made up of a certain state of acquired knowledge laid down in the course of the preceding ages and providing a ground for the more or less irregular, more or less rapid, progress of rationality; it is doubtless not even determined by what is called the mentality or the 'framework of thought' of any given period, if we are to understand by that the historical outline of the speculative interests, beliefs, or broad theoretical options of the time. This *a priori* is what, in a given period, delimits in the totality of experience a field of knowledge, defines the mode of being of the objects that appear in that field,

provides man's everyday perception with theoretical powers, and defines the conditions in which he can sustain a discourse about things that is recognized to be true. In the eighteenth century, the historical *a priori* that provided the basis for inquiry into or controversy about the existence of genera, the stability of species, and the transmission of characters from generation to generation, was the existence of a natural history: the organization of a certain visible existence as a domain of knowledge, the definition of the four variables of description, the constitution of an area of adjacencies in which any individual being whatever can find its place."

59. On a notion of the "now" derived in dialogue with non-philosophy, see Daniel Colucciello Barber, "The Immanent Refusal of Conversion," *Journal of Cultural and Religious Theory* 13.1 (Winter 2014): pp. 142–50.

60. PNP, p. 223.

61. I have placed "reality" in brackets because, while French allows for *vécu* to function grammatically as a nominative, in English "lived" is idiomatically an adverb that must be attached to a noun like "experience" or "reality." Such a mixed notion is, of course, at odds with non-philosophical language. Another way of writing such a concept in English may be "lived-reality," the hyphen used to indicate that this is a single, unified concept. While some might think this is merely a question for translators, such stylistic questions will be important for English language thinkers who want to take up non-philosophy in a more indigenous mode. Such an indigenous mode is called for since non-philosophy does not aim to subordinate a lived (life) to thought, but to render thought adequate to that lived (life): "Non-Philosophy has no identifiable effect outside of its immanent exercise, which is to use philosophy and science to render thought adequate to the *jouissance* of an eternal or immanent 'life'" (PNP, p. 230).

CHAPTER 6

1. Friedrich Nietzsche, *On the Genealogy of Morality*, ed. Keith Ansell-Pearson, trans. Carol Diethe (Cambridge: Cambridge University Press, 1997), p. 35.

2. PNP, p. 283.

3. See PNP, p. 231.

4. PhNP, p. 10 (translation slightly modified).

5. John Ó Maoilearca, "The Future of Continental Philosophy" in *The Continuum Companion to Continental Philosophy*, ed. John Ó Maoilearca and Beth Lord (London: Continuum, 2009), p. 260. Though the distinction is largely artificial, there is an ideology of the distinction that is very important for academic Anglophone philosophy. Careers literally depend upon it, though here the reign of analytic philosophy can be understood via extraphilosophical means and without a naive belief that the purity and strength of its method won out. See, for example, John McCumber, *Time in the Ditch: American Philosophy and the McCarthy Era* (Chicago: Northwestern University Press, 2001), in which McCumber argues that the seemingly apolitical nature of analytic philosophy

led to its being supported by administrators and others eager to avoid political controversy. This led in part to the anemic nature of the discipline and was ultimately responsible for a series of philosophy department closures as the relevance of philosophy as a discourse useful for social and political problems waned.

6. François Laruelle, "Is Thinking Democratic? Or, How to Introduce Theory into Democracy" in *Laruelle and Non-Philosophy*, ed. Ó Maoilearca and Smith, p. 229.

7. Ibid.

8. See my *A Non-Philosophical Theory of Nature* for an explication of the ecosystem of thought concept and the way it may be used to read the history of philosophy.

9. See Simon Critchley, *Continental Philosophy: A Very Short Introduction* (Oxford: Oxford University Press, 2001), pp. 1–11.

10. James Burton, "Research Problems and Methodology: Three Paradigms and a Thousand Exceptions" in *The Continuum Companion to Continental Philosophy*, ed. Ó Maoilearca and Lord, p. 14.

11. Readers should consult Laruelle's critique of Badiou's philosophy as authoritarian. See François Laruelle, *Anti-Badiou: On the Introduction of Maoism into Philosophy*, trans. Robin Mackay (London: Bloomsbury, 2013). I have claimed in a review essay that Badiou's philosophy is in many ways quite close to Laruelle's non-philosophy and so his critique of Badiou also operates as a self-critique of certain temptations for non-philosophy. See Anthony Paul Smith, "Review of *Anti-Badiou: On the Introduction of Maoism into Philosophy*" in *Notre Dame Philosophical Review* (4 November 2013), available online at <https://ndpr.nd.edu/news/43895-anti-badiou-on-the-introduction-of-maoism-into-philosophy> (last accessed June 12, 2015).

12. Quentin Meillassoux, *After Finitude: An Essay on the Necessity of Contingency*, trans. Ray Brassier (London: Continuum, 2008), p. 5.

13. For the best reading to date of Laruelle in relation to "speculative realism" see Galloway, *Laruelle: Against the Digital*, pp. xvii–48.

14. While Quentin Meillassoux and Iain Hamilton Grant simply have not used the term to describe themselves, Ray Brassier has done more than merely distance himself from the term, remarking in an interview that "I see little philosophical merit in a 'movement' whose most signal achievement thus far is to have generated an online orgy of stupidity." For the rest of his remarks on the "movement" see Ray Brassier, "I am a nihilist because I still believe in truth," interviewed by Marcin Rychter, *Kronos* (March 2011), available online at <http://www.kronos.org.pl/index.php?23151,896> (last accessed May 27, 2015).

15. Graham Harman, "On the Undermining of Objects: Grant, Bruno, and Radical Philosophy" in *The Speculative Turn: Continental Materialism and Realism*, ed. Bryant, Srnicek, and Harman, p. 21.

16. Graham Harman has remarked upon this via his popular blog that it would be false to imply "an obvious line of ancestry between Laruelle and all of

speculative realism." See Graham Harman, "Laruelle's 'seeming closeness to speculative realism'," Object-Oriented Philosophy (blog), 29 November 2012, available online at <https://doctorzamalek2.wordpress.com/2012/11/29/laruelles-seeming-closeness-to-speculative-realism> (last accessed June 12, 2015).

17. "Continental naturalism" strikes me as a more useful and less misleading term than "Speculative Realism." Other than Ian James, in *The New French Philosophy*, the other texts that have attempted to give an account of this post-Continental turn have largely neglected Laruelle, relegating him to footnotes regarding Brassier's work or devoting a few remarks to the potential that may lie in non-philosophy. The work of James is distinctive in so far as his overview of contemporary French philosophy is not concerned with the moniker "speculative realism" and so sees a continuity between philosophers like Nancy and Badiou that those invested in speculative realism would want to deny. Two recent texts provide deeper philosophical engagements with speculative realism, while largely ignoring the work of Laruelle. See Peter Gratton, *Speculative Realism: Problems and Prospects* (London: Bloomsbury, 2014), where the work of Meillassoux, Brassier, Grant, and Harman is discussed alongside that of the materialist philosophers Adrian Johnston and Catherine Malabou. In Steven Shaviro, *The Universe of Things: On Speculative Realism* (Minneapolis: University of Minnesota Press, 2014), we find an expansion of the sense of speculative realism, more in line with Ó Maoilearca's post-Continental philosophy and which even includes the work of Alfred North Whitehead. We find there more engagement with Laruelle as Shaviro compares him to Meillassoux, writing: "Meillassoux and Laruelle alike seek to step away from the self-confirming totalizations of correlational thought. But whereas Meillassoux radicalizes and surpasses correlationism through an exacerbated form of dialectical speculation, Laruelle instead performs a radical withdrawal from speculation" (p. 129).

18. François Laruelle, "Digital Epistolary between François Laruelle and Drew S. Burk," interview by Drew S. Burk, email (December 2012), unpublished.

19. Against the prevailing idealism present in contemporary philosophy, he writes: "Beyond the Idea, there is the real, but outside of its empirico-ideal forms, the real in the state of an a priori, an a priori that no longer takes the form of the repetition or of supplement as substitutive repetition." François Laruelle, *Le Principe de minorité* (Paris: Aubier Montaigne, 1981), p. 111.

20. Louis Morelle, "Speculative Realism: After Finitude, and Beyond? *A vade mecum*," trans. Leah Orth with the assistance of Mark Allan Ohm, Jon Cogburn, and Emily Beck Cogburn, *Speculations* III (2012): p. 251.

21. Ibid., p. 252.

22. See François Laruelle, *The Concept of Non-Photography*, trans. Robin Mackay (Falmouth and New York: Urbanomic/Sequence, 2011), and François Laruelle, *Photo-Fiction, A Non-Standard Aesthetics*, trans. Drew S. Burk (Minneapolis: Univocal Publishing, 2012).

23. Morelle, "Speculative Realism," p. 258.

24. Ibid., p. 259.
25. Ibid., p. 261.
26. Laruelle even comes to the counter-intuitive conclusion that death is not real for the human in the same sense that life is not absolute. Cf. Laruelle, *Future Christ*, pp. 101–4.
27. See Brassier, *Nihil Unbound*, pp. 138–9.
28. Morelle, "Speculative Realism," p. 265.
29. Ibid., p. 266.
30. See Iain Hamilton Grant, *Philosophies of Nature after Schelling* (London: Continuum, 2006), pp. 19–21, 194. My understanding of Grant has been greatly aided by Daniel Whistler. See his "Language after Philosophy of Nature: Schelling's Geology of Divine Names" in *After the Postsecular and the Postmodern: New Essays in Continental Philosophy of Religion*, ed. Anthony Paul Smith and Daniel Whistler (Newcastle-upon-Tyne: Cambridge Scholars Publishing, 2010), pp. 335–59.
31. Morelle, "Speculative Realism," p. 247.
32. Ibid., p. 268.
33. For a movement predicated on the acceleration of technological advances remarkably little of this work has been carried out online. See, in print, Robin Mackay and Armen Avanessian (eds), *#Accelerate: The Accelerationst Reader* (Falmouth: Urbanomic, 2014) for the core texts and claims. Brassier is counted among the main figures of the "movement."
34. For a longer version of this argument see Smith, *A Non-Philosophical Theory of Nature*, pp. 217–26.
35. Laruelle, "Non-Philosophy, Weapon of Last Defence," p. 249.
36. See IP for this argument.
37. PNP, p. 224.
38. PNP, p. 287. Elsewhere, Laruelle says that this democracy may also take the name "communism." See, NM, pp. 140–9.
39. While noesis and noema are important in the final chapter of *Principles of Non-Philosophy*, they do not recur with great intensity throughout the rest of Laruelle's corpus. Since the precise meaning of these terms is far from uncontroversial amongst Husserlian phenomenologists, I did not see great value in hastily sketching that very technical debate. Interested readers should begin with Husserl's work itself. See Edmund Husserl, *Ideas I: General Introduction to Pure Phenomenology*, trans. W.R. Boyce Gibson (London and New York: Routledge, 2012), §88.
40. Cf. PNP, p. 300.
41. See Kant, *Critique of Pure Reason*, A ix.
42. PNP, p. 265.

Bibliography

Badiou, Alain. "Interview with Ben Woodard." In *The Speculative Turn: Continental Materialism and Realism*. Ed. Levi Bryant, Nick Srnicek, and Graham Harman. Melbourne: re:press, 2011. 19–20.

—. *The Century*. Trans. Alberto Toscano. Cambridge: Polity, 2007.

—. *Being and Event*. Trans. Oliver Feltham. London and New York: Continuum, 2005.

Balibar, Étienne, Barbara Cassin, and Alain de Libera. "Subject." In *Dictionary of Untranslatables: A Philosophical Lexicon*. Ed. Barbara Cassin. Trans. David Macey. Translation edited by Emily Apter, Jacques Lezra, and Michael Wood. Princeton: Princeton University Press, 2014. 1069–91.

Barber, Daniel Colucciello. "The Immanent Refusal of Conversion." *Journal of Cultural and Religious Theory* 13.1 (Winter 2014): 142–50.

Bell, Catherine. *Ritual Theory, Ritual Practice*. Oxford: Oxford University Press, 2009.

Boulnois, Olivier. "Object." In *Dictionary of Untranslatables: A Philosophical Lexicon*. Ed. Barbara Cassin. Trans. Steven Rendall, Christian Hubert, Jeffrey Mehlman, Nathanael Stein, and Michael Syrotinski. Translation edited by Emily Apter, Jacques Lezra, and Michael Wood. Princeton: Princeton University Press, 2014. 723–7.

Brassier, Ray. "I am a nihilist because I still believe in truth." Interview by Marcin Rychter. *Kronos* (March 2011). Web. November 31, 2014. <http://www.kronos.org.pl/index.php?23151,896>

—. *Nihil Unbound: Enlightenment and Extinction*. Basingstoke: Palgrave, 2007.

Brassier, Ray, Iain Hamilton Grant, Graham Harman, and Quentin Meillassoux. "Speculative Realism." In *Collapse III*. Falmouth: Urbanomic, 2007. 307–449.

Breazeale, Daniel. "Fichte's Conception of Philosophy as a 'Pragmatic History of the Human Mind' and the Contributions of Kant, Platner, and Maimon." *Journal of the History of Ideas* 62.4 (October 2001): 685–703.

Burton, James. "Research Problems and Methodology: Three Paradigms and a Thousand Exceptions." In *The Continuum Companion to Continental Philosophy*. Ed. John Ó Maoilearca and Beth Lord. London: Continuum, 2009. 9–32.

145

Cixious, Hélène. *Portrait of Jacques Derrida as a Young Jewish Saint.* Trans. Beverley Bie Brahic. New York: Columbia University Press, 2004.

Critchley, Simon. *Continental Philosophy: A Very Short Introduction.* Oxford: Oxford University Press, 2001.

Deleuze, Gilles and Félix Guattari. *What Is Philosophy?* Trans. Hugh Tomlinson and Graham Burchell. New York: Columbia University Press, 1994.

Derrida, Jacques. "Violence and Metaphyics: An Essay on the Thought of Emmanuel Levinas." In *Writing and Difference.* Trans. Alan Bass. London and New York: Routledge, 2001. 97–192.

—. "Circumfession." In *Jacques Derrida.* Trans. Geoffrey Bennington. Chicago: University of Chicago, 1999.

Eyers, Tom. *Post-Rationalism: Psychoanalysis, Epistemology, and Marxism in Post-War France.* London: Bloomsbury, 2013.

Fichte, J.G. *Science of Knowledge.* Trans. and ed. Peter Heath and John Lachs. Cambridge: Cambridge University Press, 1982.

Foucault, Michel. *The Order of Things: An Archeology of the Human Sciences.* London: Routledge, 2002.

Galloway, Alexander R. *Laruelle: Against the Digital.* Minneapolis: University of Minnesota Press, 2014.

—. "The Autism of Reason." *Angelaki: Journal of the Theoretical Humanities* 19.2 (2014): 73–83.

Galloway, Alexander R., Eugene Thacker, and McKenzie Wark. *Excommunication: Three Inquiries in Media and Mediation.* Chicago: Chicago University Press, 2014.

Gangle, Rocco. *François Laruelle's Philosophies of Difference: A Critical Introduction and Guide.* Edinburgh: Edinburgh University Press, 2013.

Gödel, Kurt. *On Formally Undecidable Propositions of Principia Mathematica and Related Systems.* Trans. B. Meltzer. New York: Dover Publications, Inc., 1992.

Grant, Iain Hamilton. *Philosophies of Nature after Schelling.* London: Continuum, 2006.

Gratton, Peter. *Speculative Realism: Prospects and Problems.* London: Bloomsbury, 2014.

Gschwandtner, Christina M. *Postmodern Apologetics?: Arguments for God in Contemporary Philosophy.* New York: Fordham University Press, 2013.

Hallward, Peter and Konx Peden (eds). *Concept and Form, Volume 1: Key Texts from the* Cahiers pour l'Analyse. London: Verso, 2012.

Harman, Graham. "Review of François Laruelle's *Philosophies of Difference: A Critical Introduction to Non-Philosophy.*" Notre Dame Philosophical Reviews. 12 August 2011. Web. June 21, 2013. <http://ndpr.nd. edu/news/25437-philosophies-of-difference-a-criti cal-introduction-to-non-philosophy/>

—. "On the Undermining of Objects: Grant, Bruno, and Radical Philosophy." In *The Speculative Turn: Continental Materialism and Realism.* Ed. Levi Bryant, Nick Srnicek, and Graham Harman. Melbourne: re:press, 2011. 21–40.

Heidegger, Martin. "Modern Science, Metaphysics, and Mathematics." In *Basic Writings.* Trans. and ed. David Farrell Krell. New York: HarperSanFrancisco, 1993. 267–305.

Heidegger, Martin. *What Is Called Thinking?* Trans. J. Glenn Grey. New York: Harper & Row, 1968.

Henry, Michel. *From Communism to Capitalism: Theory of a Catastrophe.* Trans. Scott Davidson. London and New York: Bloomsbury, 2014.

—. *Barbarism.* Trans. Scott Davidson. London and New York: Continuum, 2012.

—. *Words of Christ.* Trans. Christina M. Gschwandtner. Grand Rapids: William B. Eerdmans Publishing Co., 2012.

—. *I Am the Truth: Toward a Philosophy of Christianity.* Trans. Susan Emanuel. Stanford: Stanford University Press, 2003.

—. *Marx: A Philosophy of Human Being.* Trans. K. McLaughlin. Bloomington: Indiana University Press, 1983.

—. *The Essence of Manifestation.* Trans. Girard Etzkorn. The Hague: Martinus Nijhoff, 1973.

Hofstadter, Douglas R. *I Am a Strange Loop.* New York: Basic Books, 2007.

—. *Gödel, Escher, Bach: An Eternal Golden Braid.* New York: Basic Books, 1979.

Horkheimer, Max and Theodor W. Adorno. *Dialectic of Enlightenment: Philosophical Fragments.* Ed. Gunzelin Schmid Noerr. Trans. Edmund Jephcott. Stanford: Stanford University Press, 2002.

Husserl, Edmund. *Ideas I: General Introduction to Pure Phenomenology.* Trans. W.R. Boyce Gibson. London and New York: Routledge, 2012.

—. *The Crisis of European Sciences and Transcendental Phenomenology: An Introduction to Phenomenological Philosophy.* Trans. David Carr. Evanston: Northwestern University Press, 1970.

James, Ian. *The New French Philosophy.* Cambridge: Polity, 2012.

Kant, Immanuel. *Critique of Pure Reason.* Trans. and ed. Paul Guyer and Allen W. Wood. Cambridge: Cambridge University Press, 1998.

Kolozova, Katerina. *Cut of the Real: Subjectivity in Poststructuralist Philosophy.* New York: Columbia University Press, 2014.

Laruelle, François. *General Theory of Victims.* Trans. Jessie Hock and Alex Dubilet. Cambridge: Polity, 2015.

—. *Introduction to Non-Marxism.* Trans. Anthony Paul Smith. Minneapolis: Univocal Publishing, 2015.

—. *Intellectuals and Power: The Insurrection of the Victim.* In conversation with Philippe Petit. Trans. Anthony Paul Smith. Cambridge: Polity, 2014.

—. "Principles for a Generic Ethics." Trans. Anthony Paul Smith. *Angelaki: Journal of the Theoretical Humanities* 19.2 (2014): 12–23.

—. *Principles of Non-Philosophy.* Trans. Nicola Rubczak and Anthony Paul Smith. London and New York: Bloomsbury, 2013.

—. *Anti-Badiou: On the Introduction of Maoism into Philosophy.* Trans. Robin Mackay. London: Bloomsbury, 2013.

—. *Philosophy and Non-Philosophy.* Trans. Taylor Adkins. Minneapolis: Univocal Publishing, 2013.

—. "A Rigorous Science of Man." In *From Decision to Heresy: Experiments in Non-Standard Thought.* Trans. and ed. Robin Mackay. Falmouth: Urbanomic, 2012. 33–74.

Laruelle, François. "Digital Epistolary between François Laruelle and Drew S. Burk." Interview by Drew S. Burk. December 2012. Unpublished.

—. "Is Thinking Democratic? Or, How to Introduce Theory into Democracy." In *Laruelle and Non-Philosophy*. Ed. John Ó Maoilearca and Anthony Paul Smith. Trans. Anthony Paul Smith. Edinburgh: Edinburgh University Press, 2012. 227–37.

—. "Non-Philosophy, Weapon of Last Defence: An Interview with François Laruelle." In *Laruelle and Non-Philosophy*. Ed. John Ó Maoilearca and Anthony Paul Smith. Trans. Anthony Paul Smith. Edinburgh: Edinburgh University Press, 2012. 238–51.

—. *Photo-Fiction, A Non-Standard Aesthetics*. Trans. Drew S. Burk. Minneapolis: Univocal Publishing, 2012.

—. *Struggle and Utopia at the End Times of Philosophy*. Trans. Drew S. Burk and Anthony Paul Smith. Minneapolis: Univocal Publishing, 2012.

—. *The Concept of Non-Photography*. Trans. Robin Mackay. Falmouth and New York: Urbanomic/Sequence, 2011.

—. *Future Christ: A Lesson in Heresy*. Trans. Anthony Paul Smith. London: Continuum, 2010.

—. *Philosophies of Difference: A Critical Introduction to Non-Philosophy*. Trans. Rocco Gangle. London and New York: Continuum, 2010.

—. *Philosophie non-standard. Générique, Quantique, Philo-Fiction*. Paris: Kime, 2010.

—. "The Truth According to Hermes: Theorems on the Secret and Communication." Trans. Alexander R. Galloway. *Parrhesia* 9 (2010): 18–22.

—. *Théorie des identités. Fractalité généralisée et philosophie artificielle*. Paris: PUF, 1992.

—. *En tant qu'Un. La « non-philosophie » expliquée aux philosophes*. Paris: Aubier, 1991.

—. *Une Biographie de l'homme ordinaire. Des Autorités et des Minorités*. Paris: Aubier, 1985.

—. *La Principe de minorité*. Paris: Aubier Montaigne, 1981.

—. *Nietzsche contra Heidegger. Thèses pour une politique nietzschéene*. Paris: Payot, 1977.

Laruelle, François and Anne-Françoise Schmid. "Sexed Identity." Trans. Nicola Rubczak. *Angelaki: Journal of the Theoretical Humanities* 19.2 (2014): 35–9.

Laruelle, Francois, Tony Brachet, Gilbert Kieffer, Laurent Leroy, Daniel Nicolet, Anne-Françoise Schmid, and Serge Valdinoci. *Dictionary of Non-Philosophy*. Trans. Taylor Adkins. Minneapolis: Univocal Publishing, 2013.

Levinas, Emmanuel. *Otherwise than Being: Or Beyond Essence*. Trans. Alphonso Lingis. Pittsburgh: Duquesne University Press, 1998.

—. *Totality and Infinity: An Essay on Exteriority*. Trans. Alphonso Lingis. Pittsburgh: Duquesne University Press, 1969.

McCumber, James. *Time in the Ditch: American Philosophy and the McCarthy Era*. Evanston: Northwestern University Press, 2001.

McGettigan, Andrew. "Fabrication Defect: François Laruelle's Philosophical Materials." *Radical Philosophy* 175 (September/October 2012): 33–42.

Mackay, Robin. "Introduction: Laruelle Undivided." In *From Decision to Heresy: Experiments in Non-Standard Thought*. Ed. Robin Mackay. Falmouth: Urbanomic, 2012. 1–32.

Mackay, Robin and Armen Avanessian, eds. *#Accelerate: The Accelerationist Reader*. Falmouth: Urbanomic, 2014.

Marion, Jean-Luc. *Descartes' Grey Ontology: Cartesian Science and Aristotelian Thought in the* Regulae. Trans. Sarah Donahue. South Bend, IN: St. Augustine's Press, 2014.

—. *God Without Being: Hors-Texte*. 2nd edition. Trans. Thomas A. Carlson. Chicago: University of Chicago Press, 2012.

—. *Being Given: Toward a Phenomenology of Givenness*. Trans. Jeffery Kosky. Stanford: Stanford University Press, 2002.

—. *On Descartes' Metaphysical Prism: The Constitution and Limits of Onto-theology in Cartesian Thought*. Trans. Jeffrey L. Kosky. Chicago: Chicago University Press, 1999.

—. *Reduction and Givenness: Investigations of Husserl, Heidegger, and Phenomenology*. Trans. Thomas A. Carlson. Evanston: Northwestern University Press, 1998.

—. *Sur la théologie blanche de Descartes. Analogie, création des vérités éternelles, fondement*. Paris: PUF, 1981.

Meillassoux, Quentin. *After Finitude: An Essay on the Necessity of Contingency*. Trans. Ray Brassier. London: Continuum, 2008.

Morelle, Louis. "Speculative Realism: After Finitude, and Beyond? *A vade mecum*." Trans. Leah Orth with the assistance of Mark Allan Ohm, Jon Cogburn, and Emily Beck Cogburn. *Speculations* III (2012): 241–72.

Nagel, Ernest and James R. Newman. *Gödel's Proof*. London and New York: New York University Press, 2001.

Neuhouser, Frederick. *Fichte's Theory of Subjectivity*. Cambridge: Cambridge University Press, 1990.

Ó Maoilearca, John. *All Thoughts Are Equal: Laruelle and Nonhuman Philosophy*. Minneapolis: University of Minnesota Press, 2015.

—. "The Animal Line: On the Possibility of a 'Laruellean' Non-Human Philosophy." *Angelaki: Journal of the Theoretical Humanities* 19.2 (2014): 113–29.

—. "The Future of Continental Philosophy." *The Continuum Companion to Continental Philosophy*. Ed. John Ó Maoilearca and Beth Lord. London: Continuum, 2009. 259–75.

—. *Post-Continental Philosophy: An Outline*. London and New York: Routledge, 2006.

Peden, Knox. *Spinoza contra Phenomenology: French Rationalism from Cavaillès to Deleuze*. Stanford: Stanford University Press, 2014.

Schmid, Anne-Françoise. "The Science-Thought of Laruelle and its Effects on Epistemology." In *Laruelle and Non-Philosophy*. Trans. Nicola Rubczak. Ed. John Ó Maoilearca and Anthony Paul Smith. Edinburgh: Edinburgh University Press, 2012. 122–42.

Schmid, Anne-Françoise and Armand Hatchuel. "On Generic Epistemology." Trans. Robin Mackay. *Angelaki: Journal of the Theoretical Humanities* 19.2 (2014): 131–44.

Shaviro, Steven. *The Universe of Things: On Speculative Realism.* Minneapolis: University of Minnesota Press, 2014.

Smith, Anthony Paul. "François Laruelle." In *Religion and European Philosophy: Key Thinkers from Kant to Today.* Ed. Philip Goodchild and Hollis D. Phelps. London and New York: Routledge, forthcoming.

—. "Review of *Anti-Badiou: On the Introduction of Maoism into Philosophy.*" Notre Dame Philosophical Reviews. 4 November 2013. Web. November 31, 2014. <https://ndpr.nd.edu/news/43895-anti-badiou-on-the-introduction-of-maoism-into-philosophy/>

—. *A Non-Philosophical Theory of Nature: Ecologies of Thought.* New York and London: Palgrave Macmillan, 2013.

—. "Thinking from the One: Non-Philosophy and the Ancient Philosophical Figure of the One." In *Laruelle and Non-Philosophy.* Ed. John Ó Maoilearca and Anthony Paul Smith. Edinburgh: Edinburgh University Press, 2012. 19–41.

Smith, Daniel W. "The Doctrine of Univocity: Deleuze's Ontology of Immanence." In *Deleuze and Religion.* Ed. Mary Bryden. London: Routledge, 2001. 167–83.

Whistler, Daniel. "Language after Philosophy of Nature: Schelling's Geology of Divine Names." In *After the Postsecular and the Postmodern: New Essays in Continental Philosophy of Religion.* Ed. Anthony Paul Smith and Daniel Whistler. Newcastle-upon-Tyne: Cambridge Scholars Publishing, 2010. 335–59.

Zahavi, Dan. *Husserl's Phenomenology.* Stanford: Stanford University Press, 2003.

Index